The Friends' Book

FOR THE FRIEND WHO'S

Best AT Everything

ALISON MALONEY

Michael O'Mara Books Limited

First published in Great Britain in 2009 by
Michael O'Mara Books Limited
9 Lion Yard
Tremadoc Road
London SW4 7NQ

A CIP catalogue record for this book is available from the British
Library.

Papers used by Michael O'Mara Books Limited are natural,
recyclable products made from wood grown in sustainable forests.
The manufacturing processes conform to the environmental
regulations of the country of origin.

ISBN: 978-1-84317-359-5

1 2 3 4 5 6 7 8 9 10

www.mombooks.com

Cover design by Blacksheep Design
Designed and typeset by K.DESIGN, Winscombe, Somerset
Illustrations by Robyn Neild

Printed and bound in England by Clays Ltd, St Ives plc

For Debbie, Karen, Sally, Joss, Rob and
Sarah, for being great pals.

Contents

CONTENTS

Introduction

This is a book for the person you turn to when things get tough, the person you call when you finally find that perfect pair of shoes and who, above all, is there for you in any crisis, day or night: in short, a true friend.

Here is a collection of wit and wisdom for the friend who's best at everything. It's full of practical advice, from how to throw your best chum an amazing birthday party to breaking the news that her new dress is two sizes too small, and crammed with tips on everything from shopping to being a good listener, true stories, jokes, cocktail recipes and much, much more.

Good friends make the bad times bearable and give the good times that extra sparkle – because, as a wise man once said, we all need someone to lean on. But being the friend who's best at everything is darn hard work . . . so put your feet up, have a chocolate biscuit, and read on.

'A friend is known when needed.'
ARABIAN PROVERB

'Friendship makes prosperity more brilliant,
and lightens adversity by dividing and sharing it.'
CICERO, ROMAN PHILOSOPHER, ORATOR
AND STATESMAN (106 BC–43 BC)

The Companion Set

We choose our close friends for their individual personalities and, consequently, we often call on them at different times. For example, the pal we turn to in a crisis is not necessarily the first one we'd choose when we fancy a wild night out. Here is the essential set of companions for every woman. But which one are you?

THE GOSSIP

She's the one in the know and she's always prepared to share. She can't wait to get you on the phone and bend your ear on the latest scandal; she can put an outrageous spin on any story, and is always guaranteed to keep you amused with the very latest rumours.

MOST LIKELY TO SAY: 'You'll never guess what she's done this time!'

LEAST LIKELY TO SAY: 'Nothing much has happened this week.'

PROS: Top marks for entertainment value.

CONS: You'll have to keep your deepest, darkest secrets to yourself.

'There is only one thing in the world worse than being talked about, and that is not being talked about.'
OSCAR WILDE, NOVELIST, PLAYWRIGHT AND WIT
(1854–1900)

THE BITCH

She never has a kind word to say about anyone – except you, of course. She can be hilarious when being cruel about other people and she is always likely to cheer you up if you're feeling down.

MOST LIKELY TO SAY: 'What DOES she look like in that dress?'

LEAST LIKELY TO SAY: 'She's such a lovely person.'

PROS: Everyone likes a bitching session every now and then.

CONS: If she can be catty about others behind their backs, she's a dead cert to do the same to you.

THE LISTENER

You can often tell who your closest friend is by asking yourself who you would turn to in your darkest hour. This girl is the obvious answer because she's caring, generous and willing to lend a sympathetic ear and a shoulder to cry on, any hour of the day or night.

MOST LIKELY TO SAY: 'I'll come over right away and you can tell me all about it.'

LEAST LIKELY TO SAY: 'Pull yourself together and get over it!'

PROS: She's steadfast, solid and dependable.

CONS: Tea and sympathy is not necessarily the best thing to get you out of the doldrums.

THE PARTY GIRL

She's fabulous on a night out, fantastic fun to be around and always up for a laugh. The minute the sun goes down, she's up for anything and she won't tolerate a party-pooper. If you want to paint the town red, she'll bring the brushes.

MOST LIKELY TO SAY: 'Let's get this party started!'

LEAST LIKELY TO SAY: 'I fancy a night in.'

PROS: You'll always have a great time with her in tow.

CONS: If you fancy an early night or a quiet weekend, she'll never let you forget it.

Honour Bestowed

When your best friend is approaching those happy milestones of life – getting married, having a baby, embarking on a new career – she's bound to be over the moon, but she'll still need plenty of your support. She may have dreamed of walking down the aisle since she was knee-high to a grasshopper but having a true best friend around to take care of the nitty-gritty (like holding onto the train so she doesn't trip head-first into the altar) is essential to making it the best day of her life. Being asked to take an important role in a friend's milestone moment is a fantastic thrill – a confirmation that she loves and trusts you above all others – but do be prepared to work hard, be organized and stay very calm in the face of adversity, over-excitement and sometimes lots of booze.

BEING A BRIDESMAID

BE RESTRAINED: You may instantly think, when being invited to be a bridesmaid, that this is your chance to enjoy a night of drinking, dancing and flirting with the groomsmen in a fabulous frock – but hold your horse and carriage! Remember this is your friend's day, not yours. Your job is to be a graceful, demure addition to the wedding party, not to knock back the champers from dusk till dawn and be immortalized with a goofy grin in your best friend's precious wedding photos. Indulge in a drink or two when it's appropriate during the course of the day – during the girly getting-ready phase and for each toast to the bride and groom after the speeches – but have a non-alcoholic drink after each tipple to remain clear-headed. You can really let your hair down when your duties are well and truly over.

BE DIPLOMATIC: If your friend saddles you with a corker of a dress (shiny unflattering fabric, puffy sleeves, all covered in bows) keep all your criticisms to yourself and smile on regardless as you slip into your burgundy court shoes. This is not the time to question her fashion sense and besides, everyone knows that a bride outshone by a bridesmaid is a very unhappy bride indeed. Let her bask in her celestial beauty, and, God willing, she'll do the same for you when it comes to your big day.

> 'Kindred spirits are not so scarce as I used to think.
> It's splendid to find out there are so many of them in
> the world.'
> **ANNE, FROM *ANNE OF GREEN GABLES***
> **BY L. M. MONTGOMERY (1874–1942)**

THE BEST WOMAN FOR THE JOB

It's more and more common these days for brides to choose a Best Woman to lean on as they prepare to say 'I do'. If a groom can pick a best friend to get them to the church on time, why shouldn't the bride get the same helping hand? This is an honour to cherish but it does require you to hold on to a cool head when your normally rational pal has become a Bridezilla

of gigantic proportions. She needs you to tell her everything is going to be just fine, even if the florist has turned up with the wrong colour roses and the pageboy has rubbed chocolate into his white shirt. Take the strain for her on this day and she'll treasure the memories for a lifetime.

BE PREPARED: Before the big day, write up a list of where everyone is supposed to be and when. Make copies for the rest of the wedding party and marshal everyone to where they should be. Be ruthlessly bossy with dawdlers to make sure everyone is seated for the big bridal entrance. Ahead of time, put together an emergency fix-all kit: needle and thread, headache tablets, small scissors and chewing gum. Tucked away in your handbag, it will be a discreet lifesaver should any small hiccup come your way.

> 'Without friends no one would choose to live,
> though he had all other goods.'
> ARISTOTLE, GREEK PHILOSOPHER (384 BC–322 BC)

BE YOURSELF: If you're asked to deliver a speech, don't panic. It's not your job to thank everyone or be hilariously funny (the Best Man should carry that burden). Write a speech from the heart: tell everyone how you met your best friend, what she means to you and how happy you are that she's met the man of her dreams. If you give a speech that's relaxed and heartfelt you'll find that all the nerves slip away when you stand up in front of the reception guests.

Harry: 'You realize, of course, that we could never be friends.'
Sally: 'Why not?'
Harry: 'What I'm saying is – and this is not a come-on in any way, shape or form – is that men and women can't be friends because the sex part always gets in the way.'
FROM THE FILM *WHEN HARRY MET SALLY* (1989)

BE SELFLESS: It may be your job to squeeze in an extra place setting, pour countless glasses of bubbly and chat happily to a near-deaf great-aunt while all your other friends are tearing up the dance floor. While you might be tempted to pout, just remember that your friend chose you for this important role because she trusts you completely and you'll be the one she thanks for years to come. Treat the service and reception like an event you're organizing at work: tidy up any problems as you go and chat to everyone as you meander around. At the end of the night, hang up your heels with the satisfaction that you've done your BF proud as the ultimate go-to girl.

A HEAVENLY GODPARENT

BE RESPECTFUL: You might not be a very religious person, but if your friend is holding a christening or other significant ceremony for their precious newborn, you can bet they are, so be respectful of their beliefs. If you don't know much about their faith system, why not get in touch with whoever will lead the ceremony and find out all about it? Your commitment will be really appreciated.

BE A GROWN-UP: Agreeing to help nurture and mentor a child is a job for life, so make sure you treat the ceremony with the sensitivity it deserves. No mucking about with the font water as you promise to help teach your best friend's offspring right from wrong! If you do feel the giggles coming on, just take a deep breath and clear your head.

BE IN IT FOR THE LONG-HAUL: Being a godparent goes beyond the church doors; get as involved as you can with your godchild's upbringing. On their birthday each year, why not collect a classic book that you loved as a child so that by the time they get to grips with reading there will be a library of favourites to share with them? Alternatively, put away a little money into a savings account in their name each year so when they turn seventeen you can surprise them with a full course of driving lessons or a computer to take away to university. A little forward planning early on can lead to a huge surprise in later years. Not only will your friend appreciate your help but, in taking up an active role in their child's life, you have cemented your relationship as their lives take on a more domestic direction. And you'll have a brand-new little friend thrown into the bargain!

Put Your Money Where Your Mouth Is

British author and politician Joseph Addison once lent a good friend some money to tide him over in hard times. A few weeks later Addison noticed that, whereas in the past when he and his friend discussed worldly matters they always used to disagree on various subjects, now his friend was agreeing with everything he said. One day, Addison decided to choose a subject on which he knew that his friend held a completely opposing view from him, saying, 'Either contradict me, sir, or pay me my money!'

A TEST OF CHARACTER

BE A GOOD REFERENCE: If your best friend has asked you to provide a winning reference for an exciting new job, take the task in hand as seriously as you would if it was *your* career in the balance. They're asking you because they rate you as a best friend who'll do them proud, so don't run the risk of slipping up by being too casual or under-prepared.

BE STUDIOUS: Make sure you get all the details of the job so you can tailor your reference to best show off their skills to fit that role. Do they need to come across as organized, a team player, a natural leader, a go-getter? Also write down the dates of previous jobs so you don't umm and ahh while giving the reference over the phone, or make a mistake when typing one up.

BE FAIR: If you rave on about how fabulously amazing and perfect your friend is without giving practical examples, you don't give a prospective new boss much to go on, except that you can be a bit of a chatterbox. Think of their three best skills to talk about and try not to go over the top with pointless praise. A new boss won't be sold on your best friend's ability to make a lovely shepherd's pie but they may be impressed to hear about any big social events they've organized or volunteer work they're doing.

Be a Friend

Be a friend. You don't need money:
Just a disposition sunny;
Just the wish to help another
Get along some way or other;
Just a kindly hand extended
Out to one who's unbefriended;
Just the will to give or lend,
This will make you someone's friend.

FROM 'BE A FRIEND' BY EDGAR A. GUEST (1881–1959)

How to Make Friends and Influence People

It's a fact: you can never have too many friends. But it's also a fact that it's very easy to slip into the same old patterns, year in, year out, and you might realize that you spend most of your time with the same handful of people. It's never too late to get out there and find new friends. You never know what sort of diverse and fascinating people you'll come across and how they'll challenge you and support you in ways you didn't even know you were missing. Here are some ideas of new hobbies and activities that will throw you into the path of like-minded new friends, as well as just being damn good fun and easy to slot into your busy schedule.

ARE YOU SPEAKING MY LANGUAGE?

Learning a new language is not only a great way to meet a new bunch of people and get to know them at each lesson, but it'll also revive those grey cells from going totally grey. You'll get a boost of confidence from your new skill and with your new classmates you can sit in the local pub and discuss *EastEnders* in fluent Spanish, impressing all the locals. You'll meet people from all walks of life who are learning a new language for all sorts of reasons, some who might be emigrating to a foreign country. Who knows, if you're friendly enough, you might just be rewarded with an invitation to stay in their Tuscan villa . . . But learning something new does take commitment and time, so make sure you'll be able to make each lesson and do your homework in between.

> 'A friend is one to whom one may pour out all the contents of one's heart, chaff and rain together, knowing that the gentlest of hands will take and sift it, keep what is worth keeping and, with a breath of kindness, blow the rest away.'
> ARABIAN PROVERB

THE FULL HOUSE

Poker is back with a vengeance and bigger than ever, with high profile celebrities joining the circuit as well as the traditional high rollers. However, you needn't book a flight to Vegas just yet; there are plenty of local and regional poker clubs that welcome beginners and new members. There are pub poker nights too, often with only a couple of pounds buy-in, so you don't feel under too much pressure. As well as being great fun and a chance to meet new people, it'll sharpen your wits and teach you some excellent card-sharp skills that'll impress your other mates the next time the cards come out. In fact, why not take a group of friends and get chatting to some regulars to get tips? Make sure you do this in the breaks between a game though, because the serious players won't take kindly to being

distracted. You never know, you might just get lucky and win the pot – but the golden rule is never bet more than you can afford to lose.

WE'RE GOING TO NEED CONSIDERABLY BIGGER BUNS

A pastime traditionally associated with the more mature lady is joining the Women's Institute. However, the WI has had a bit of a facelift recently and with home sewing and knitting all the rage once more, where better to hone your crafty skills than with a bevy of like-minded ladies? You'll find great tips on everything culinary and domestic, plus you can attend talks by visiting experts on all sorts of things, from flower arranging to car maintenance. The Women's Institute is a wealth of clever female know-how just round the corner, so look up your nearest branch on the Web and get making that jam!

Jokes to Share with Friends

What do you call a woman who knows where her husband is every night?

A widow.

A friend of mine got her contraceptive pills mixed up with her valium.

She has twelve kids but she really doesn't care!

Why did God make Eve?

Because he took one look at Adam and thought, 'I must be able to do better than that.'

Why are married women heavier than single women?

Single women come home, see what's in the fridge and go to bed. Married women come home, see what's in bed and go to the fridge.

True Friends

'I have lost friends, some by death, others through sheer inability to cross the street.'
VIRGINIA WOOLF, NOVELIST AND
FEMINIST (1882–1941)

GREATER LOVE HATH NO WOMAN . . .

As two women walked into a medical centre in New Jersey, they caught each other's eye and giggled. It was a perfect demonstration of the sense of humour that had bound them together for forty years as best friends. Together they were laughing in the face of an enormous ordeal. One of these ladies was about to risk her life to save her best friend.

Patty Hurley and Eileen Riley had met at high school and had shared a close bond ever since, through marriage, children and divorce. But when Eileen, a nurse, was diagnosed with kidney disease, she didn't go running to her friend – Patty came to her, ringing to find out what was wrong after hearing Eileen was sick.

'My kidneys are failing,' Eileen explained.

'Can I give you one of mine?' came the instant response.

It was such a casual offer, that Eileen thought she had heard wrong but timidly broached the subject again at the end of the call. Patty confirmed what she had said and that she meant every word, and their journey to the operating table began.

After tests, the women were found to be a good match.

'I never once hoped I would find out I couldn't do it,' said Patty. 'In fact, the more I learned, the more I wanted to do this.'

And Eileen never doubted her friend's commitment saying simply, 'She makes a promise, she keeps it.'

The operation went ahead in November 2008, and both women are now fighting fit and closer than ever.

'There are no words to describe how amazing this woman is,' Eileen said afterwards. 'She gave me my life.'

> 'Friendship . . . is not something you learn in school.
> But if you haven't learned the meaning of friendship,
> you really haven't learned anything.'
>
> MUHAMMAD ALI, LEGENDARY WORLD
> HEAVYWEIGHT CHAMPION BOXER

LIFELONG FRIENDS

As World War I ended in 1918 a remarkable friendship was formed between two little girls. New next-door neighbours Vera Turner and Dorothy Luxton hit it off immediately, and ninety years on, in 2008, they celebrated Christmas together as Britain's oldest friends.

The steadfast friends first met at the age of three, in their home town of Sidmouth, Devon, then went to the local school together. They attended cookery classes together at the age of fifteen and both wed in 1939. Vera (née Anstis) married a local butcher and stayed in Sidmouth, while Dorothy (née Gaut), wed a munitions worker who became a civil servant and moved

away. They kept in regular contact, despite the distance between them, and both had three children.

When Dorothy's husband, Peter, retired they moved back to the town and built a house next door to Vera!

By Christmas 2008 the pair were both widowed great-grandmothers and Vera celebrated her ninety-third birthday on Boxing Day.

'I have so many fond memories of us as little girls playing games together,' she said. 'We would do skipping, hoops – the blacksmith would make us an iron hoop – and hopscotch in the road; there were no cars going through the village then.'

It wasn't always easy to get together when Dorothy was living away from Devon, but they made sure they kept in contact.

'Dorothy used to come visiting, but not a lot in those days because it was more difficult to travel,' Vera explains. 'We would keep in touch with letters and cards while she was away.'

After they were reunited they made a regular date every Saturday to walk along the seafront together to buy an ice cream, and they put their long lives down to plenty of exercise.

'We are more like sisters really,' says Vera. 'I have always enjoyed walking and we would go on lots of walks together. We had a lot of fun.'

> 'I count myself in nothing else so happy
> As in a soul remembering my good friends.'
> FROM *RICHARD II* BY WILLIAM SHAKESPEARE
> (*c.*1564–1616)

BEYOND THE CALL OF DUTY

American travel writer Bill Bryson once told of his great friendship with producer Allan Sherwin, whom he met for a drink one night, just before setting off for a trip to Australia. 'I mentioned', wrote Bryson, 'my plans on the next trip to tackle the formidable desert regions alone . . . In order to deepen his admiration for me, I had told him some vivid stories of travellers who had come unstuck in the unforgiving interior. One of these had pertained to an expedition in the

1850s led by a surveyor named Robert Austin, which grew so lost and short of water in the arid wastes beyond Mt. Magnet in Western Australia that the members were reduced to drinking their own and their horses' urine. The story affected him so powerfully that he announced at once the intention to accompany me through the most perilous parts of the present trip, in the role of driver and scout.' As reported, Sherwin did join Bryson on a later trip to Northern Queensland where, very generously, he told Bryson, 'I just want you to know that if it comes to it you may have all of my urine.'

Keep it Kind

Constructive criticism is all very well, but don't take a leaf out of Joan Rivers's book. Her best pal Elizabeth Taylor has had to endure some pretty cutting comments about her well-known weight issues.

'When I took her to Sea World and Shamu the Whale jumped out of the water,' Joan once declared, 'she asked if it came with vegetables!'

On another occasion Joan quipped, 'She's so fat, she's my two best friends.'

A FRIEND IN NEED

Childhood pals Tara Sturman and Andrea Cobbold gave birth to children within five months of each other. Less than a year later they went under the knife to save the lives of their babies – both born with the same rare condition.

The mums, who live in Suffolk, donated part of their livers to save ten-month-old India and thirteen-month-old Alex in 2007, in an operation that had only been carried out a handful of times before.

The children were diagnosed with biliary atresia, which affects just fifty babies in England and Wales each year and, if unchecked, leads to liver poisoning and cirrhosis.

Although Andrea wouldn't wish the ordeal on her friend, she was grateful they have been able to turn to each other. 'It's a staggering coincidence that Tara had to go through the same ordeal. It's an emotional time. Having a close friend who knows exactly what you're going through is an enormous help.'

> 'Friendship is born at that moment when one person says to another, "What! You too? I thought I was the only one."'
> C. S. LEWIS, NOVELIST (1898–1963)

I'D DO ANYTHING . . .

In 2002, actress Marisa Tomei was in the Bahamas with a bunch of girlfriends. While swimming at the plush resort where they were staying, Marisa was stung on the arm by a venomous Portuguese man-of-war jellyfish.

The lifeguard suggested she go straight to a doctor and told her the sting would be itchy and sore for days. One of her pals, however, had a more natural remedy – and obligingly peed on the actress's arm. The sting was gone within twenty-four hours.

The Best Fictional Friends

Sherlock Holmes and Doctor Watson
Peter Pan and Wendy
Piglet and Pooh
Charlie Brown and Snoopy
Lone Ranger and Tonto
Tom Sawyer and Huckleberry Finn
Jack and Jill
Sooty and Sweep
Tom and Jerry
Asterix and Obelisk

Pampered Pals

A pamper day at a health club is all very well but they don't come cheap. Instead, turn your living room into a home spa and have hours of fun sharing beauty tips and treatments for a lot less cash.

Get some snacks, some beauty products and an oil burner to set the mood, and indulge yourselves.

MANICURE MANIA

Who needs a nail technician when you have each other? Pool your resources by getting your guest or guests to bring along their nail varnishes, nail kit and plenty of varnish remover in case it all goes horribly wrong!

Basic Manicure

YOU WILL NEED:
Nail files
Orange sticks
Cotton buds
Nail polish remover and cotton wool balls
Bowl of warm, soapy water or cuticle cream
Towels
Hand cream or coconut oil
Base coat or strengthener
Top coat
Nail varnish

① Remove traces of any previous nail varnish.

② Choose your shape by looking at the length of your fingers. Long, elegant hands look great with long nails but short, stubby fingers should have an oval nail that is no more than 3 or 4 mm (¼ inch) past the fingertip.

③ File with an emery board. Always file in one direction only, not in a sawing motion. Use the rougher side to shorten the nail and the finer side to shape.

④ Soak hands in a bowl of warm, soapy water for two minutes, then, using a cotton bud or orange stick, gently push back the cuticles. Alternatively, use a cuticle cream before gently pushing them back.

⑤ Massage the hands with hand cream or coconut oil for a few minutes, to increase circulation and moisturize the skin.

⑥ Use a cotton bud dipped in remover to take the cream/oil off the nails.

⑦ Apply a clear base coat or strengthener to the nails. This will prevent any coloured nail polish staining your nails.

⑧ When the base coat is dry, apply coloured varnish, starting with one stroke at the centre of the nail and then one stroke on either side.

⑨ Wait until it is completely dry then apply a second coat.

⑩ Finish with a top coat to protect from chipping.

'I believe in manicures. I believe in overdressing.
I believe in primping at leisure and wearing lipstick.
I believe in pink. I believe that loving is the best calorie burner.
I believe in kissing. I believe that happy girls are the prettiest girls.
I believe that tomorrow is another day and I believe in miracles.'
AUDREY HEPBURN, AMERICAN ACTRESS (1929–1993)

Going French

YOU WILL NEED:

Nail guides, or guide strips, available from chemists
and supermarkets
White nail varnish
Pale pink or natural-tone nail varnish
(You can also buy French manicure kits that contain
everything required.)

A French manicure is a two-tone look with white nail tips and pink, or light beige, on the rest of the nail. It works well for short to moderate-length nails.

① Follow steps 1 to 6 above and then apply a base coat.

② Stick a tip guide onto each nail. This covers the lower part of the nail, leaving the tip uncovered.

③ Apply white nail varnish to the exposed tips.

④ Wait until the white is dry, remove the tip guide and then paint the entire nail with the pale pink or natural beige colour. Apply a second coat if necessary.

⑤ Finish with a glossy top coat.

Eugh!

Suzie and her pal were on a fitness drive and decided to go swimming together. After getting out of the pool and showering, the two women were dressing in the communal changing room when her friend started looking around her in a puzzled fashion.

'I can't find my knickers anywhere,' she said, so Suzie obligingly helped her search.

As they looked, Suzie, who was already fully dressed, opened her swim bag and found, to her horror, that her own underwear was still inside. Realizing she was wearing her pal's knickers, she hastily shut her bag and said innocently, 'I can't find them anywhere!' Her friend was forced to go home commando!

FACE IT TOGETHER

Face masks and scrubs are wonderful beauty fixes and a whole lot of fun to share. You can make your own masks and treatments from the contents of your fridge and fruit bowl as so many natural foods have great rejuvenating qualities. Be careful though – if you are allergic to eating it, don't put it on your skin, as it could all go horribly wrong!

One essential ingredient for a fun pamper night is a camera. Who can resist taking a picture of the best mate when her face is covered in strawberry mush or green slime? Your social-networking site awaits!

Banana and Honey Mask

Good for dry skin, as it has great moisturizing properties.

① Mix half a mashed banana with 1 tablespoon honey and 2 tablespoons sour cream or natural yoghurt.

② Smear all over face and leave for ten minutes.

③ Rinse off with warm water.

Simply Avocado Mask

This versatile fruit (yes, it is a fruit not a vegetable) is full of vitamins A, D and E, which are great for the skin.

① Mash the flesh of 1 ripe avocado and spread over face.

② Leave for 20 minutes

③ Rinse with warm water, then cold water to close the pores.

'Friendship is precious, not only in the shade, but in the sunshine of life, and thanks to a benevolent arrangement the greater part of life is sunshine.'

THOMAS JEFFERSON, THIRD PRESIDENT OF THE UNITED STATES (1743–1826)

Yeast Mask

A good cleansing mask for oily skin.

① Mix 1 teaspoon of brewer's yeast and 1 tablespoon of plain yoghurt.

② Apply to the oiliest areas of the skin and leave for 15–20 minutes.

③ Rinse with warm water, then cold water to close the pores.

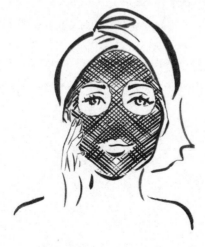

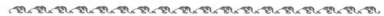

Oatmeal Scrub

A great exfoliant for dry skin.

① Mix 1 tablespoon of oats with 1 teaspoon of baking soda.

② Add water to make a paste.

③ Rub gently over skin and then rinse with warm water.

Sugar Babe Mask

This is a great-wrinkle buster for more mature skin.

① Dissolve 3 tablespoons of sugar in 4 tablespoons of warm water then wash your face with the solution.

② Wipe off with a warm flannel.

> 'It's so much more friendly with two.'
> **WINNIE-THE-POOH, FROM *POOH'S LITTLE INSTRUCTION BOOK* INSPIRED BY A. A. MILNE (1882–1956)**

Friendship Groups

'Each friend represents a world in us, a world possibly
not born until they arrive, and it is only by this meeting
that a new world is born.'
FROM THE JOURNALS OF ANAÏS NIN,
FRENCH-CUBAN-SPANISH AUTHOR (1903–1977)

Everybody has different friends from different walks of life.
Whether you first met in your work canteen or on the first day
of nursery, it's worth indulging in some bonding now and again
to remind each different kind of friend how glad you are of the
role they play in your life – and you'll be having a good time,
thrown into the bargain!

NINE-TILL-FIVE FRIENDS

It's easy sometimes to overlook those people that you see day
in day out, but work friends can, without you even realizing,
become best friends. They hear all those details of your life in
daily conversation and they really are the best people with
whom to share work stresses, as they do know exactly what
you mean. It's worth putting a little more effort into these
friendships, as having a bounce in your step when you walk
into your office is absolutely priceless and any boring old job is
cheered up by having fun, caring people to do it with. Why not
start a bowling team at work and play once a fortnight, or start

a cake club where you take it in turns to bake a cake on a Friday? Or have work friends round to your home for a pot-luck dinner party and swap favourite recipes (though you must be kind about any dishes that weren't exactly favourites!).

A+ FRIENDS

It's your oldest friends that can sometimes make you feel youngest at heart. Never mind if you have a mortgage, two kids and a flashy career, your school friends know who you first snogged behind the chemistry lab and when you tried your first Malibu and coke. It's an event in itself just to get together and relive old times, so all you need to do is chill the wine, lay out the nibbles and get the nostalgia going. Why not have an evening when you gather together all your old school photos and discuss your awful uniforms and haircuts? Or put together a compilation CD of the tunes you were dancing to at your leavers' school disco and throw some shapes around the living room together. It may feel like you've known these girls forever but going that extra mile will make sure you're still top of the class in their eyes for years to come.

'A faithful friend is the medicine of life.'
THE BIBLE, ECCLESIASTICUS CH.6, V.16

FAR AND AWAY FRIENDS

If a best friend has to move away for a great new job or a serious relationship, it can feel like it's the end of the line as far as your friendship is concerned. But with the wide range of snazzy, mostly free technologies available it really doesn't have to be. Why not arrange a time each week when you'll both be online (if your friend is in another time zone, make sure to compensate for this – her 6 p.m. might be your 4 a.m.!) and catch up on everything via instant messenger or a webcam through a network like Skype? You can carry on your gossip sessions and show off your latest purchase, just as you would if she was in the same room. Letters and small tokens sent through the post are always well received and let your friend know you're thinking of her even though you're miles away.

HAPPY FAMILIES

If you're lucky enough to have siblings close in age, then chances are you're likely to have a ready-made bunch of best friends. But don't overlook other members of your family who can also become great friends and not just people to whom you send Christmas cards with a gift token inside. Your aunts, uncles, cousins and nieces and nephews will all have lots in common with you, and will give you a chance to blow off steam away from your immediate family. Popping round to visit your granny or great-aunt can reveal lots of quirks and anecdotes you didn't know about your heritage, plus all sorts of useful old-fashioned tips about mending clothes, growing plants and cooking. Why not organize a huge family reunion with long-lost branches of the family? You'll probably discover you have distant relations in all walks of life and end the evening with a whole new bunch of friends-in-the-making.

> "'I don't want him," said Rabbit. "But it's always useful to know where a friend-and-relation is, whether you want him or whether you don't."'
> FROM *THE HOUSE AT POOH CORNER*
> BY A. A. MILNE (1882–1956)

MIXING IT UP

Having a big party can sometimes throw up big worries: not only about whether everyone will come, but also will they all get on? It feels like a daunting task to introduce friends from different areas of your life that so far have stayed in their own little worlds, but if you do you'll find it's a lot easier than it seems. Firstly, everyone there has one big thing in common: they are there for *you*. They think you're the bee's knees and will want to make a good impression on your other friends for your sake. Secondly, they're going to be just as keen to meet new, funny and interesting people at a party as you are, so all you have to do is introduce people with the odd bit of trivial information, such as where they've just been on holiday, or any famous person they may have met, and let the conversational chemistry do its thing. Gather together a few party games to have in reserve, just in case, but trust in the fact that if you think all these people are great fun, they're bound to get on well together.

Too Many Friends?

Normally, people think that there's no such thing as having too many friends, but this was not something that seemed to bother Max Beckmann – the early-twentieth-century German Expressionist artist. The professors at the university at which Beckmann was lecturing wanted to throw a party in his honour, and so sent an emissary over to the Beckmanns' house to proffer their invitation. Answering the door, Mrs Beckmann said she had better just check with her husband, only to return a few minutes later to say that the answer was, 'No, thank you. He has enough friends already!'

Unusual Friendships

Friendship can spring up in the most unlikely places and between widely differing personalities. Here is a collection of famously unusual friendships that bridge all sorts of divides – class, temperament and even oceans.

GERTRUDE STEIN AND ERNEST HEMINGWAY

At the time they met, Hemingway was only twenty-two and had been invited to the Paris salon of Stein, then forty-seven and a well-respected connoisseur of the arts. The pair took an immediate shine to each other and gradually Stein became a mentor for the young writer. It was, in fact, Stein who first suggested that Hemingway should visit Spain and who introduced him to bullfighting.

GROUCHO MARX AND T. S. ELIOT

The American comedian and Nobel Prizewinning poet kept up a long-standing correspondence and their touching and often hilarious letters have been widely published. Their correspondence was a source of mutual pride: Eliot had a portrait of Marx (requested) proudly displayed in his home and Groucho summed up their interest in one another with his trademark wit: 'I had read up on T. S. Eliot, "Murder In The

Cathedral" and a few things like that, and I thought I'd impress him. And all he wanted to talk about was the Marx Brothers. That's what happens when you come from St. Louis.'

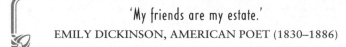

'My friends are my estate.'
EMILY DICKINSON, AMERICAN POET (1830–1886)

HELENE HANFF AND FRANK DOEL

Helene Hanff, an avid book collector and writer from the USA, and Frank Doel, chief buyer for the London bookseller Marks & Co., kept up a twenty-year friendship by correspondence which was later chronicled in Hanff's book *84 Charing Cross Road*. Sadly, Doel died before Hanff had a chance to visit him and his family in London. Her book was made into a film adaptation of the same name starring Anthony Hopkins in 1987.

JOHN HENRY 'DOC' HOLLIDAY AND WYATT EARP

Wyatt Earp, famous for the gunfight at the OK Corral, had this to say of his tuberculosis-ridden friend: 'Doc was a dentist, not a lawman or an assassin, whom necessity had made a gambler; a gentleman whom disease had made a frontier vagabond; a philosopher whom life had made a caustic wit; a long lean ash-blond fellow nearly dead with consumption, and at the same time the most skilful gambler and the nerviest, speediest, deadliest man with a gun that I ever knew.'

'Health is the first good lent to men;
A gentle disposition then:
Next, to be rich by no by-ways;
Lastly, with friends t' enjoy our days.'
ROBERT HERRICK, ENGLISH POET (1591–1674)

QUEEN VICTORIA AND JOHN BROWN

Queen Victoria became reclusive after the death of Prince Albert in 1861, spending more and more time in the tranquillity of her Scottish estate at Balmoral. There she became firm friends with her plain-speaking manservant John Brown. Speculation about the romantic nature of their relationship was rife, but the rumours were never confirmed. Their friendship was the subject of the 1997 film *Mrs Brown*, starring Judi Dench and Billy Connolly.

THE LADIES OF LLANGOLLEN

This was the nickname given to Lady Eleanor Butler and the Hon. Sarah Ponsonby, who in the late eighteenth century scandalized their families and much of the nation by running away together and setting up home in Wales, rather than be forced into dreary marriages of convenience. Their families more or less cut them off without funds, but in the end they became famous for their courageous stand against the mores of the time, and were visited by, among others, Wordsworth, Byron, Shelley, Lady Caroline Lamb, Wellington, Scott and Wedgwood. Eventually Queen Charlotte persuaded George III to grant them a pension.

Friends in High Office

One of the many jobs US President Abraham Lincoln had to deal with every week was the appeals for pardon that came to him from soldiers who were due to be disciplined by the military. As a matter of precedent, each appeal usually came with a bundle of letters from the man's friends and other people of influence in support of him. However one day an appeal landed on Lincoln's desk with nothing attached. 'What!' the President is said to have shouted, 'Has this man no friends?' When the President heard that the man was indeed friendless, he replied, 'Then I will be his friend,' and signed a pardon.

Surprise!

Next time your pal has a special birthday coming up, plan the whole event for her. If you are good at keeping secrets you could make it a surprise do, but be careful that your cover story is watertight. It's no good telling her you're busy that night and hoping she won't organize something else, because she will. What's more, she'll be disappointed in you and will end up feeling pretty down if she thinks no one cares enough to celebrate with her. Tell her you are taking her for a pizza or to the pub. Just keep the fact that all her family and friends will be there a secret and make sure they don't blow it.

CELEBRATE IN STYLE

If your mate has a big birthday coming up and you fancy splashing some cash, club together with some others and hire some transport with a difference. Forget the limo – what about a fire engine? A few old vehicles have been converted with luxury seats and champagne buckets in the back and your very own fireman in the driving seat! Other themed limos for hire include prison vans, police cars and ambulances. Or, if you're after something a bit more unusual, what about hiring a classic car and a chauffeur to take her and a select group of friends out for cocktails at a swanky hotel?

THIS IS YOUR LIFE PARTY

Get out the big red book of memories and give her a surprise by inviting all those friends she's lost touch with, or hardly ever sees – providing she doesn't actually hate them. Start with a small group of her friends and family and then introduce a couple of old primary school pals, or the childhood crush who moved away. As each person enters the room, get them to tell a story about your friend. It takes a lot of organization, so don't leave it until the last minute. It's worth it though – you'll have a blast and she'll never forget it!

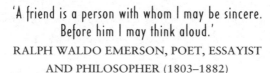

'A friend is a person with whom I may be sincere.
Before him I may think aloud.'
RALPH WALDO EMERSON, POET, ESSAYIST
AND PHILOSOPHER (1803–1882)

CHOCOLATE HEAVEN

No girly night is complete without the sweetest ingredient of all, and what better way to serve it than out of an irresistible flowing fountain. If you want your pal to keep it as a gift (or you want one for yourself), you can buy a relatively cheap chocolate fountain. For a more luxurious version, hiring is more cost-effective and your package will include all the chocolate (which will be of the highest quality), as well as the marshmallows, strawberries, mini-doughnuts and all the other dippers required. As a bonus, you won't have the horrendous job of cleaning out the machine afterwards.

If the gathering is more intimate, why not substitute the fountain for a chocolate fondue. If you have, or can borrow, a fondue set, this is a great dessert for friends seated round a table. If you can't get hold of one, don't worry, you can use a heavy-bottomed saucepan, but it will help if you have a warming plate to put it on as you dip – otherwise you'll have to wolf it down before it sets!

Chocolate Fondue Recipe

As well as a fondue set or heavy saucepan, you will need skewers or dipping forks.

INGREDIENTS:
> Selection of foods to dip in the fondue, e.g. fruit cut into chunks, marshmallows, amaretti biscuits or mini meringues
> 400–500 g (14–18 oz) good quality plain chocolate (at least 70 per cent cocoa solids)
> 100 ml (3 fl oz) double cream
> 2 tablespoons brandy (optional)

① Prepare the items for dipping and place into separate bowls.

② Break the chocolate into chunks, place in the fondue pan (or saucepan) and melt over a very low heat, stirring with a wooden spoon.

③ When the chocolate is just melted, add the double cream and stir in.

④ Place the fondue pan on the lit warmer (or the saucepan on the plate warmer) and serve immediately with the bowls of things to dip.

> 'Go through your phone book, call people and ask them to drive you to the airport. The ones who will drive you are your true friends. The rest aren't bad people; they're just acquaintances.'
>
> JAY LENO, AMERICAN COMIC AND TALK-SHOW HOST

GIFT GODDESS

The usual smellies and chocolates are great presents, but not from your closest pal. You are the one who knows her best so you should be able to pick the perfect present every time. Go for the unexpected, as long as you know that she'll love it.

Here are some ideas:

Entertainment Value

Tickets to see a band you both really love or a film or play that you're both dying to see is a great idea. How about taking her to the reunion tour of a cheesy band you loved years ago. That way you get a bit of nostalgia and share a few laughs into the bargain.

Curtains Down

Hungarian playwright Ferenc Molnár sat down with a friend to watch a particularly bad play. He had been given free tickets by the management and it would have been churlish not to go. However, his good manners soon failed him and by the end of the first scene he stood up to leave. His shocked friend whispered 'We're guests!' and Molnár sat back down for a few more moments before starting up again. When his friend asked him where he was going, he replied 'To the box office; to buy tickets so we can leave.'

Trip Down Memory Lane

Nothing bonds us together more than a shared memory. Buy a photo album and go through your own photo collection, filling the album with pics of the great times you've spent together. Add funny little comments and include mementoes such as film tickets or beer mats picked up along the way. You'll both have so much fun going through it and she'll love her unique gift.

Perfect Pottery

Don't fork out on a cheesy mug with 'Best Friend' and a cutesy teddy bear on it – design your own. You can buy paint-your-own mug, bowl and plate kits for very little money in toy shops, craft shops and large newsagents. Better still, find a local pottery studio or café where you can paint your own design on a vast array of pottery products and have it professionally glazed. You can use a nickname you have for her, paint a picture or just write a funny message. It will be such a personal gift that she will treasure it always (and probably be too scared to use it!).

> 'This is the way I see it; good friends offer to help in a crisis, great friends don't take no for an answer.'
> BREE VAN DE CAMP, FROM TV SERIES
> *DESPERATE HOUSEWIVES*

Make it Happen

Pick an activity she has often said she would like to try, and book it. If she has expressed an interest in scuba-diving, water skiing or driving a racing car, the chances are she will never get round to it herself. But you could book a one-off lesson for her and go along for moral support.

A Giving Gift

Is your friend the girl who has everything, including a heart of gold? Instead of spending your hard-earned cash on a useless nick-nack, do something worthwhile. If she is an animal lover, you can sponsor an endangered animal through various protection charities, such as the WWF (World Wildlife Fund). To help a poor community in the developing world you can buy a chicken or a goat, or farming tools, and if she is an eco warrior, have a tree planted in her name.

The Cherry on the Cake

Show you care with a home-made cake for her birthday. After all, anyone can buy a cake but only a special friend puts time and effort into baking one. She'll be touched. For the theme, think about her favourite leisure activities, cartoon characters or hobbies. For example, if she is a fanatical fashionista, try a designer handbag design. If she is soppy about soccer, a football pitch and miniature players, and so on. Cupcakes are also a great idea, as they are easy to bake and look fabulous when decorated with a few different coloured toppings and decorations.

The Gift of Poetry

One day the poet Thomas Gray and a friend attended a book sale, at which a beautifully crafted bookcase containing a rare collection of leather-bound French classics caught Gray's attention. 'Why don't you buy it?' his friend asked, to which Gray replied that he would but that he couldn't afford the one hundred guineas' asking price. Unbeknown to Gray, the Duchess of Northumberland overheard this conversation and asked Gray's friend the identity of the man who was so interested in the bookcase, and subsequently bought the object herself. Later that day there was a knock at Gray's door and, much to his surprise, there on the pavement stood the bookcase he had so coveted. Attached to it was a note apologizing for making so tiny a gesture in return for the immense pleasure the Duchess had gained from reading Gray's 'Elegy Written in a Country Churchyard'.

The Danger Zone

'If it's painful for you to criticize your friends – you're
safe in doing it. But if you take the slightest pleasure in
it – that's the time to hold your tongue.'
ALICE DUER MILLER, AMERICAN POET (1874–1942)

Like a good marriage, every friendship has their ups and downs
but if your relationship is a strong one, it will weather the
storm. To help you avoid the stickiest of situations, here is a
guide to the most common breaking points and the golden rules
that will save you from falling out for good.

HOLIDAYS

You know you and your pal get on like a house on fire, you
love going to the same places and doing the same things, but is
that enough? However close you are, the first time you spend
a week or a fortnight in each other's company 24/7 can prove
a difficult test. Remember that some people behave very
differently when they are away from home, especially if they
are abroad, and too much hot sun and alcohol can strain the
best of bonds.

'A friend is one soul inhabiting two bodies.'
ARISTOTLE, GREEK PHILOSOPHER (384 BC–322 BC)

THE SOLUTION:

Before you commit to a holiday, have a good think about any traits that might annoy you and decide if you can live with them for a week or two. Lay down some ground rules, and make sure she knows where your boundaries are and listen to any concerns she may have too. Then enjoy yourself!

A NIGHT OUT

Opposites attract and just because you are close doesn't mean you love doing the same things all the time. Clubbing every night might be your idea of fun, but is it hers? Being dragged along on someone else's idea of a great night out can cause

resentment and, if you throw alcohol in the mix, things can get messy.

THE SOLUTION:

If she suggests a night at the cinema or a quiet drink, don't bully her into doing what you fancy. Instead, take it in turns to choose the kind of evening you will have and the venue.

> 'Love is blind; friendship closes its eyes.'
> FRENCH PROVERB

FLAT SHARES

Who could be a better flatmate than your best friend? Moving in together can be the perfect solution to a housing crisis, and shared rent means more cash in your pocket. But will you still love her as much when you get home from work, dying for a cuppa, and she's nicked the last of the milk? Or you get up for work and she's borrowed your best suit without asking? Her obsessive tidiness or slovenly laziness might be the butt of your jokes when you live apart but will drive you nuts when it affects your space too.

THE SOLUTION:

Before moving in together, draw up a list of house rules and stick to them. Decide whether you will have a joint housekeeping pot, or will only buy your own food. If it's the latter, keep separate cupboards in the kitchen and have separate shelves in the fridge. Work out a cooking and cleaning rota so that each of you does your fair share. Finally, stick to renting. Buying a property with a friend can be a nightmare and a joint mortgage will become a millstone around your neck if one of you decides to settle down with a partner.

Winds of Change

Sometimes one's friends can abandon one, which is precisely what happened to Jacques Soustelle when he was governor general of Algeria for a year during the 1950s. Writing to the French President, Charles de Gaulle, Soustelle complained that all of his friends were attacking him for supporting de Gaulle's policies in Algeria. Back came the succinct, if rather unhelpful, reply, '*Changez vos amis*' ('Change your friends').

THIRD WHEEL

It's likely that at some point one of you will be single while the other settles down with a partner. Suddenly, she isn't on the end of the phone every time you want to speak to her, can't come out every weekend with you and won't be able to drop everything and dash to your side in a crisis. Likewise, if you're the one getting serious, she will be feeling abandoned and rows can easily erupt.

THE SOLUTION:

There is no easy solution to this one, but it can be resolved with some effort and understanding on both sides. If you're the one on your own, you're going to have to accept that your friend has other commitments, branch out and find new hobbies and friends. If you're the one who has settled down with a long-term partner, make sure you regularly set aside quality time to spend with your pal and never let her feel abandoned, even if you don't have so much free time for her as you used to.

On Friendship

And a youth said, Speak to us of Friendship.
And he answered, saying:
Your friend is your needs answered.
He is your field, which you sow with love and reap with thanksgiving.
And he is your board and your fireside.
For you come to him with your hunger, and you seek him for peace.

When your friend speaks his mind you fear not the 'nay' in your own mind, nor do you withhold the 'ay'.
And when he is silent your heart ceases not to listen to his heart;
For without words, in friendship, all thoughts, all desires, all expectations are born and shared, with joy that is unclaimed.

FROM *THE PROPHET*, BY KAHLIL GIBRAN 1883–1931)

Famous Friends in Literature

WINNIE-THE-POOH and THE HOUSE AT POOH CORNER
by A. A. Milne

Christopher Robin's rag-tag collection of friends in the Hundred-Acre Wood certainly make an odd bunch – portly Pooh, timid Piglet, down-in-the-dumps Eeyore and bouncy Tigger – but they are dedicated friends to the end, capturing the spirit of childhood friendships. They can make a game out of anything on summer days that feel like they'll never end, even a popped balloon and an empty honey pot. Sharing a silly joke with an old friend can sometimes make you feel like you're instantly young again, with the whole of the summer holidays stretched out in front of you. If you're looking to rekindle that tingle of nostalgia from when you were small enough to believe in Heffalumps and Woozles, then dip into one of these classic children's books by A. A. Milne.

> MEMORABLE QUOTE:
>
> Winnie-the-Pooh: 'If you live to be a hundred, I hope I live to be a hundred minus one day, so I never have to live without you.'

'When we honestly ask ourselves which person in our lives means the most to us, we often find that it is those who, instead of giving much advice, solutions, or cures, have chosen rather to share our pain and touch our wounds with a gentle and tender hand. The friend who can be silent with us in a moment of despair or confusion, who can stay with us in an hour of grief and bereavement, who can tolerate not knowing, not curing, not healing and face with us the reality of our powerlessness, that is a friend who cares.'

HENRI NOUWEN, DUTCH PRIEST AND WRITER

(1932–1996)

EMMA by Jane Austen

Reading *Emma* is the ultimate lesson in how *not* to matchmake your friends. (If you've picked it up as a reading group book then well done you! If you haven't had the chance yet, this won't spoil it for you too much, promise.) In trying to find a perfect partner for her best friend, Harriet, Emma in fact just manages to embarrass, confuse and upset her good friend, as well as doing serious damage to her own love life. Emma and Harriet are a perfect pairing: Emma is witty and sharp where Harriet is sweet and caring. In the course of their budding

friendship they learn to adopt the other's best characteristics; by the end of the novel Emma has learned to be a bit more sensitive and Harriet has the confidence go after the things – and the man – she really wants. *Emma* is a great example of how friends can sometimes make mistakes and fall out, but ultimately the special bond that links them will always draw them back together.

MEMORABLE QUOTE:
> Mr Knightly to Miss Fairfax: 'Business, you know, may bring you money, but friendship hardly ever does.'

Bookish Friends

Meeting Dr Johnson one day in a London bookshop, James Boswell – who at the time was a lawyer – cultivated the meeting until the two men had become firm friends. Some time later they travelled together to Scotland, prompting Boswell to write of their journey in a *Tour of the Hebrides* (1785). Later still, Boswell wrote his famous biography of Johnson, which was published in 1791.

BRIDGET JONES' DIARY and BRIDGET JONES: THE EDGE OF REASON by Helen Fielding

Bridget's core of singleton best friends – Shazza, Jude and Tom – form the ultimate urban family in these books much worshipped by women of all ages. They have an opinion on everything: her clothes, her boyfriends, her bad choices and her successes. And though their friendship may be fuelled by lots of vodka and bitching, Bridget can always count on them through thick and thin. These three BFs stuck with her through the mourning periods for dead relationships, the failed diets, even the brief spell in prison . . . proving that blood may be thicker than water, but nothing's stronger than a Bloody Mary poured by a caring best friend.

MEMORABLE QUOTE:
> Bridget: 'Tom has a theory that homosexuals and single women in their thirties have natural bonding: both being accustomed to disappointing their parents and being treated as freaks by society.'

A MIDSUMMER NIGHT'S DREAM
by William Shakespeare

Helena and Hermia are such close friends even their names sound alike, but in one of Shakespeare's most famous comedies they fall into a common friendship trap and let a man come between them. These two usually demure and refined ladies resort to an all-out catfight of name-calling and hair-pulling in a competition to win the attentions of Lysander and Demetrius. But after a few interventions from the forest fairy folk and a night to sleep it off, the girls wake up with torn clothes, sore heads and apologies for each other. Remember, one man is never worth the loss of a great friend, and you might not have the benefit of magical helpers to right your wrongs . . .

MEMORABLE QUOTE:
> Helena on Hermia: 'O, when she's angry,
> she is keen and shrewd!
> She was a vixen when she went to school;
> And though she be but little, she is fierce.'

AND IT'S GOODNIGHT FROM HIM:
THE AUTOBIOGRAPHY OF THE TWO RONNIES
by Ronnie Corbett

You couldn't find a better example of a lasting and successful friendship than that of Ronnie Barker and Ronnie Corbett, aka 'The Two Ronnies'. These British national treasures entertained the nation as a best friend double-act for more than forty years, without a cross word between them. Ronnie Corbett has recorded his recollections of their time together and plenty of celeb anecdotes in this charming memoir. Perfect if you've ever laughed at 'Fork Handles'. Or should that be 'Four Candles'? This book reminds you how much laughter good friends bring into your life, comedians or not.

MEMORABLE QUOTE:
> Ronnie Corbett on Ronnie Barker: 'Pure gold in
> triplicate – as a performer, a writer and a friend.'

Animal Magic

ELEPHANT HERO

Eight-year-old Amber Miles was thrilled when she discovered the hotel where she was spending Christmas 2004, in the Thai resort of Phuket, had a special attraction. Two baby elephants, named Ning Nong and Yong were regular visitors to the beach and on Christmas Eve she ran down to the beach to see them.

A shy child, Amber hung back as others crowded around, but Ning Nong singled her out.

'When Amber first saw Ning Nong she held back as the other children crowded around,' recalled her dad Eddie, in the Channel 5 documentary *Animal Heroes*. 'Then he extended his trunk to her as a kind of invitation.'

'He gave me a big kiss on the cheek,' added Amber. 'He was very playful and kind and I fell in love with him.'

Little did she know that, two days later, her new friendship would save her life.

On Boxing Day morning, the little girl ran down to the beach to see the young elephant, leaving her parents in the hotel. Ning Nong was behaving strangely, according to his handler, and didn't want to stay on the beach.

'I was riding Ning Nong and noticed that the sea had gone out really far,' said Amber. 'Ning Nong kept heading off the beach but was brought back by Yong.'

When the sea ebbed out suddenly Ning Nong took action. With Amber on his back he fled to higher ground shortly before the devastating tsunami claimed thousands of lives.

After the first tidal wave hit, Amber's distraught mum Sam was combing the beach for signs of her daughter when she spotted her coming back. With warnings of another wave about to hit, they fled back to the hotel.

The next day she was reunited with her hero. 'He picked me up and gave me a kiss,' she said. 'And he wrapped me in his trunk.'

The resort of Phuket was one of the worst-hit areas in the disaster, with five thousand killed and thousands more reported missing.

Thanks to her animal friend, Amber returned safely to her family.

'I'll never forget Ning Nong,' says Amber. 'His quick actions saved my life.'

ANIMAL SANCTUARY

The devastating 2004 tsunami also hit the Kenyan coast and left a baby hippo stranded on a coral reef and separated from his parents. Rescued by villagers with fishing nets, the frightened animal, now named Owen, was moved to an animal sanctuary in Mombasa, where he was put in a large enclosure with two ponds in which to recover.

The enclosure was already home to a 130-year-old tortoise named Mzee and keepers at the park expected the pair to ignore each other. Instead, a remarkable friendship developed as the wise old tortoise began to look after his young companion.

'We thought we'd be feeding him and looking after him,' said Dr Paula Kahumba, director of Haller Park sanctuary. 'What happened was the opposite. Who'd have thought a young hippo would be adopted by an old tortoise? But that's what happened.'

Mzee seemed to realize that the hippo needed parental guidance and began to show him how to forage for food, where to sleep and how to survive. Owen began to mimic the movements of his adopted dad, who even taught him to swim by nudging him into one of the ponds and climbing in himself.

'Owen wouldn't eat anything at first,' explained Paula. 'Then he would follow Mzee and eat what he ate. This is probably what they do in the wild; they would follow the mother and do what they do, and that's how they learn what they should be eating.'

Owen often sleeps with his head on the tortoise's leg and the pair have even developed their own language, making similar sounds in what appears to be a conversation.

And the bond is even more amazing considering that a previous encounter with a hippo, who decided to use him as a football, resulted in Mzee's shell cracking.

'It's a miracle really, because if you try to connect them as species you cannot find a connection,' marvelled the park's vet, Dr Kashmiri. 'Obviously it's just a genuine love for each other.'

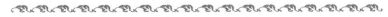

FEATHERED FRIEND

In the natural order of things, a hungry cat would look on a nearby bird as lunch. But one kitten in Massachusetts wouldn't dream of harming her best friend, who happens to be a crow.

The unlikely duo were spotted and filmed by a cat-loving couple for eight months. Amazingly, the bird would dig worms out with her beak and feed them directly to the ravenous kitten. The pair went everywhere together and would play endless games on the lawn, teasing and cajoling each other and even play-fighting.

When the fascinated couple put a dish of food out for the cat, who they named Cassie, the animal amigos would share it. And when Cassie grew brave enough to come into their home for a night's shelter in the warm, the crow would sit on the windowsill waiting for her pal to come out again. In the morning, she would greet Cassie at the top of the porch steps and the reunited duo would walk down the steps together to get on with their daily routine.

A local vet, who observed the phenomenon, believes that the motherless kitten may well have died if it had not been for her feathered friend.

'The cat, it is well to remember, remains the friend of man because it pleases him to do so and not because he must.'
CARL VAN VECHTEN, AMERICAN WRITER AND
PHOTOGRAPHER (1880–1964)

Chick Flicks and Cocktails

Jazz up the traditional DVD fest by combining it with a cocktail party and conjuring up some fantastic snacks to go with your popcorn. The great thing about a girly night with a good movie is that it is just as much fun for two as for twenty.

Many supermarkets and off-licences sell miniature bottles of speciality cocktail ingredients, such as blue curaçao and grenadine, which means you won't have to splash out on huge bottles if you want to try a few different concoctions.

For the full experience, mix your cocktails to match your movie. Here is a selection of the best chick flicks, along with some fabulous cocktail recipes to sip while you watch them:

BEACHES (1988)

Just like the friendship between the two main characters, this film stands the test of time. Bette Midler play the role of CC Bloom, a brassy, Bronx-bred entertainer whose friendship with San Francisco socialite Hillary Whitney Essex (played by Barbara Hershey) stems from a chance childhood meeting. Thirty years on she drives across the country to be with her pal when she needs her most. A real tear-jerker, so make sure your shopping list includes tissues.

MEMORABLE LINE:

CC Bloom (Midler): 'But enough about me, let's talk about you . . . what do *you* think of me?'

Companion cocktail: Beachcomber
1 tablespoon of sugar, sprinkled onto a plate
15 ml (½ oz) lime juice
Lime wedge
60 ml (2 oz) light rum
1 teaspoon cherry liqueur
1 teaspoon cherry brandy

Rub the rim of a cocktail glass with the lime wedge before dipping the glass into the plate of sugar. Put some ice cubes into a shaker with the rum, cherry liqueur, cherry brandy and lime juice. Shake well and pour into the sugar-frosted glass.

> 'My mother used to say that there are no strangers, only friends you haven't met yet. She's now in a maximum security twilight home in Australia.'
> DAME EDNA EVERAGE, AUTHOR AND TV HOST

MAMMA MIA! (2008)

The best ever feel-good movie for a girly get-together. It's got lifelong friends, gorgeous men, a potential wedding and, as if that wasn't enough, it has Abba songs. Meryl Streep plays Donna, whose daughter is getting married and wants her dad to give her away. Trouble is, there are three candidates for the

position and Donna hasn't seen them since her daughter was born.

MEMORABLE LINE:
> Donna (Streep): 'Somebody up there has got it in for me. I bet it's my mother.'

Companion cocktail: Dancing Queen
    30 ml (1 oz) banana liqueur
    30 ml (1 oz) melon liqueur
    30 ml (1 oz) cranberry juice
    30 ml (1 oz) pineapple juice

Shake ingredients together with ice and pour into a cocktail glass.

Web of Friends

'You have been my friend. That in itself is a tremendous thing. I wove my webs for you because I liked you. After all, what's a life, anyway? We're born, we live a little while, we die. A spider's life can't help being something of a mess, with all this trapping and eating flies. By helping you, perhaps I was trying to lift up my life a trifle. Heaven knows anyone's life can stand a little of that.'

FROM *CHARLOTTE'S WEB* BY E. B. WHITE (1899–1985)

SOME LIKE IT HOT (1959)

Goofy, cross-dressing comedy starring Marilyn Monroe at the height of her fame. Joe (played by Tony Curtis) and Jerry (Jack Lemmon) are musicians who mistakenly witness a mob hit. To escape the mobsters they go on the run, dressing as women (Josephine and Daphne respectively) and joining an all-girl band on tour. One of the (unusually beautiful) band-members is Sugar Kane (Monroe) and both Joe/Josephine and Jerry/Daphne fall in love with her: mistaken identities, confusion and hilarity ensue as the friends battle it out for her affections. A must-see film – for Monroe's famous wiggle, if nothing else.

MEMORABLE LINE:
Sugar (Monroe): (*Singing*) 'I wanna be loved by you, just you, nobody else but you. I wanna be loved by you alo-o-one. Boop, boop-e-doo.'

Companion cocktail: Fizzy Blonde
    30 ml (1 oz) pastis (e.g. Pernod or Ricard)
    60 ml (2 oz) advocaat
    120 ml (4 oz) lemonade

Pour the pastis and advocaat into a tall glass with ice and then add the lemonade.

FRIED GREEN TOMATOES (1991)

Unhappy housewife Evelyn Couch (played by Kathy Bates) meets Ninny (Jessica Tandy) an old lady at a retirement home, while visiting relatives. Ninny regales her with inspiring stories of the women she used to know in her younger days, and as their friendship deepens Evelyn learns to be more a more self-assured happier woman.

MEMORABLE LINE:
    Ninny (Tandy): 'I found out what the secret to life is: friends. Best friends.'

Companion cocktail: Bloody Mary
    60 ml (2 oz) vodka
    120 ml (4 oz) tomato juice
    Juice of 1 lime
    1 teaspoon Worcestershire sauce
    4 dashes Tabasco sauce
    A pinch of salt

Pour vodka, tomato and lime juice into a shaker with ice and shake vigorously. Strain onto ice cubes in a tall glass. Add the Worcestershire sauce, Tabasco and salt to taste.

Hollywood 'friends'

Infamously, Hollywood film producer Samuel Goldwyn did not get on too well with that other lion of Hollywood, Louis B. Mayer. One day, in the locker room of the Hillcrest County Club in Los Angeles, it was said that Mayer, having cornered Goldwyn, subsequently pushed him into a laundry basket. Later on, a friend commented on the incident to Goldwyn, saying how disappointed he was that the two men didn't get on. Goldwyn was apparently astonished, '*What*?' he gasped. 'We're like friends! We're like brothers! We love each other! We'd do anything for each other. We'd even cut each other's throats for each other!'

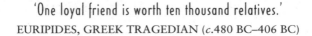

'One loyal friend is worth ten thousand relatives.'
EURIPIDES, GREEK TRAGEDIAN (*c*.480 BC–406 BC)

GONE WITH THE WIND (1939)

This is a film that has it all – flouncy dresses, tea parties, civil war and . . . Clark Gable. Headstrong Scarlett O'Hara (played by Vivien Leigh) has her heart set on marrying weak-willed Ashley Wilkes and is devastated when he marries her cousin Melanie instead. When the American Civil War breaks out and living conditions become hard, an unlikely bond of friendship develops between fiery Scarlett and kind, gentle Melanie. The love interest comes in the form of dashing and roguish Rhett Butler (played by dashing and roguish Clark Gable). Make sure you have a large box of soft tissues to hand for the weepy parts, and prepare to be stirred as you listen to the magnificent soundtrack.

MEMORABLE LINE:
Scarlett (Leigh): 'Rhett, if you go, where shall I go? What shall I do?'
Rhett (Gable): 'Frankly, my dear, I don't give a damn.'

Companion cocktail: Deep South
45 ml (1½ oz) dark rum
1 tbsp molasses
100ml (3 oz) pineapple juice
2 dashes cherry syrup

Blend ingredients in a cocktail shaker. Pour into a glass filled with ice and garnish with a pineapple wedge or pineapple chunks.

STEEL MAGNOLIAS (1987)

A magnificent cast, including Sally Field, Julia Roberts, Dolly Parton, Olympia Dukakis and Shirley MacLaine, star in a moving story of friendship in small-town Louisiana. Despite their many differences the women who meet at the local beauty parlour, run by Parton's character Truvy, have an unbreakable bond that will see them through their most tragic times. Don't rent this one if you don't want your friends to see you cry.

MEMORABLE LINE:

Ouiser (MacLaine): 'I'm not crazy, I've just been in a very bad mood for the last forty years!'

Companion cocktail: Louisiana Lullaby
45 ml (1½ oz) dark rum
3 drops of Grand Marnier
30 ml (1 oz) Dubonnet Rouge

Mix the ingredients together with ice and then strain into a cocktail glass.

> 'It's the friends you can call up at 4 a.m. that matter.'
> MARLENE DIETRICH, GERMAN-BORN ACTRESS
> (1901–1992)

SEX AND THE CITY: THE MOVIE (2008)

Four friends, girly chats, high fashion and fabulous shoes – what more could you want? Carrie, Samantha, Charlotte and Miranda bring their small-screen relationship to the big screen and throw in a wedding for good measure.

MEMORABLE LINE:

Miranda (Cynthia Nixon), drinking a Cosmopolitan: 'Why did we ever stop drinking these?'
Carrie (Sarah Jessica Parker): 'Because everyone else started!'

Companion cocktail: Cosmopolitan
  30 ml (1 oz) vodka
  15 ml (½ oz) triple sec
  15 ml (½ oz) lime juice
  15 ml (½ oz) cranberry juice
  Lime wedge

Shake the ingredients with ice in a cocktail shaker. Strain into a martini glass, garnish with a lime wedge on the rim and serve.

A True Friend is Someone Who . . .

- you can ring at three in the morning just because you feel lonely

- you can tell your secrets to, no matter how embarrassing

- can always make you laugh, no matter how sad you are

- will go on a diet with you, even though she doesn't need to

- has seen you at your very best, and your very worst

- you can share a companionable silence with, as well as chatting for hours

- knows exactly what to get for your birthday without asking

- will lend you her last fiver to buy that must-have top

- has enough embarrassing stories about you to blackmail you for the rest of your life

- and will tell you, gently, that your bum *does* look big in that.

Lady Sings the Blues

If your friend is having a rough time of it, you may not have it in your power to solve her problems, but you can listen, sympathize and help her through whatever it is she is going through.

BE PROACTIVE

Saying 'If there's anything I can do, let me know,' may be heartfelt but it doesn't cut the mustard for a true friend. She might be reluctant to ask for real help in case it is inconvenient for you. Instead, try and work out what she might need and offer specific favours. For example, if she is ill, offer to do her shopping for her, or drive her to the hospital. If it's a relationship problem, offer to take her out or just spend time with her.

'Some people go to priests; others to poetry; I to my friends.'
VIRGINIA WOOLF, NOVELIST AND FEMINIST (1882–1941)

BE BOSSY

That doesn't mean you need to bully her into submission, but if she needs organizing, or won't accept the help that she clearly needs, you may need to be a bit stronger than normal. Don't fall out with her but don't take no for an answer either.

BE SENSITIVE

Whatever your friend is going through, whether it be problems at work, a relationship break-up or a bereavement, it will affect her response to you. Think carefully about what you say and keep your cool if she snaps at you or behaves oddly. Strong emotions affect everybody in different ways, so don't judge the way she deals with her situation by your standards.

Also understand that while she appreciates your company, she might want to be alone sometimes as well.

BE PATIENT

In a traumatic or upsetting time it's hard to think of anything else, so the problem can become an obsession. Conversation may seem a bit one-sided and your friend may not realize that she has been talking about the same thing, over and over again, for months. Keep listening and eventually even she will get bored with the subject, then she'll know it's time to move on.

> 'Friendship with oneself is all-important, because without it one cannot be friends with anyone else in the world.'
> ELEANOR ROOSEVELT, FIRST LADY OF
> THE UNITED STATES (1884–1962)

BE PRACTICAL

Clear thinking is now your department. Help her by considering her situation in everything you do. For example, if she has financial issues, don't suggest a day out shopping or a trip to an expensive restaurant to cheer her up. Suggest a night in at your house instead, then go through some other ways she can save cash. If her problem is an insanely jealous boyfriend, encourage her to see sense and dump him but don't make matters worse by pressuring her into a wild night on the town against her will.

BE THERE

The most important thing a friend can do when times are tough is stick around. Be at the end of the phone when she needs you and make extra effort to pop round and see her. Put off other plans, wherever practical, if she calls in distress and needs to talk. If you live some distance away, arrange a weekend trip to see her as soon as you can and give her something to look forward to.

'Friends show their love in times of trouble.'
EURIPIDES, GREEK TRAGEDIAN (*c.*480 BC–406 BC)

What not to say:

Time is a great healer.
In a couple of years you'll look back and laugh.
There are plenty more fish in the sea.
I never liked him much anyway.
I told you so.
You should never have bought that car/house/holiday.
I know how you feel.
It's only money.
God, you look awful.
You think you've got problems!

CHEERING HER UP

Cash in the Attic

Financial problems are a huge downer and the more you sit around and think about them, the worse they seem to get. Take your pal in hand and plan a rummage day. Together you can go through all her stuff, making a pile of those things she no longer wants or needs that might be of use to someone else. Then get on to an auction website, or get a stall together at a car boot sale, and sell it. Not only will you have a lot of fun going through her old things and finding keepsakes, photos and the like, but she will feel that you are both doing something practical to help her situation.

Other ways to help are to sit down with her and write a list of her income and expenditure and work out where she can cut back. Encourage her to call her bank or loan company and arrange a sensible monthly payment for her debt, or find her a debt adviser.

Sea Breeze

Reclaim a bit of your childhood with a trip to the nearest seaside. It's still an inexpensive way to have a great day and you could go the whole hog by taking buckets and spades and making sandcastles as well as treating yourself to the obligatory ice cream and bag of chips.

The Best Medicine

You can't beat a good laugh to lift the spirits so treat her to a comedy club night. These days they don't have to be expensive and you can usually find a pub in the area with a comedy night or open-mike event. If you happen to be a bit of a comedian, you can make her laugh even more by braving the mike yourself!

Desert Island Friends

Three friends, a blonde, a brunette and a redhead, are stranded on a desert island. They find a genie's lamp and agree they'll each get one wish. The brunette and the redhead both wish they were at home and, in a puff of smoke, they're whisked away.

'Wow,' says the blonde, rubbing the lamp. 'I'm kinda lonely. I wish my friends were here!'

Makeover Magic

Looking great gives a girl a boost, especially if she is having man trouble. Grab your other mates, some beauty products and pop round to her house with hair straighteners at the ready to give her a style change. Rifle through her wardrobe and find some fab clothes she never wears, or let her borrow some of yours. If you can afford it (or you happen to be a hairdresser) treat her to a haircut. Alternatively, march her off to the nearest department store for a make-up MOT. Streaked mascara and a runny nose are not a good look, so pretty much anything you do will be an improvement.

Pyjama Party

When was the last time you had a sleepover? You don't have to be thirteen to enjoy slobbing out together, chatting, watching a movie and eating ice cream. Get plenty of midnight snacks in, put on your best PJs and have a thoroughly girly night.

> 'Stay is a charming word in a friend's vocabulary.'
> LOUISA MAY ALCOTT, AMERICAN NOVELIST AND
> AUTHOR OF *LITTLE WOMEN* (1832–1888)

Survival Kit

Make a funny survival kit for your pal. Buy a gift bag and stuff it with goodies and items that will make her laugh, to see her through her difficult time. For a break-up, include some bath salts and shampoo (so she can wash that man right out of her hair), some chocolates or sweets, a picture of her favourite film and any items that will bring a smile to her face. Include some creative elements, such as a beautifully handwritten list of 'Ten Reasons to Be Happy' – e.g. more evenings to spend with her friends, no more smelly socks to put in the wash, watch what you want on TV. Or you could include 'Night Out Vouchers' promising a trip to the movies, a night of dancing or a meal out, for her to use when she wants a good time.

Whatever is getting her down, tailor the contents to her situation and her personality.

All the Fun of the Fair

Who can be miserable on a rollercoaster? Can anyone ride a bumper car without smiling? Whether you choose a theme park or a local funfair, rides are the perfect antidote to the blues. Go wild, eat candyfloss, ride the ghost train and giggle at the hall of mirrors. It can't fail to cheer her up.

Love Fest

Sometimes we all need reminding how many people care about us. Ask your fed-up friend out for a meal and then surprise her by gathering those who love her the most. It can be just pals or you can include family, depending on how well everyone gets on. Invite a wild card to spice things up – like an old pal she's lost touch with.

> 'Misfortune shows those who are not really friends.'
> ARISTOTLE, GREEK PHILOSOPHER (384 BC–322 BC)

A Girl's Gotta Shop

CARRIE: 'Honey, if it hurts so much, why are
we going shopping?'
SAMANTHA: 'I have a broken toe, not a broken spirit.'
FROM THE TV SERIES *SEX AND THE CITY*

Most of us lack the cash that the *Sex and the City* ladies splash, but shopping can still be something of a ritual to us girls. For a great day out, what can beat a huge shopping centre, a close pal and a yummy lunch in between?

THE GOLDEN RULES OF SHOPPING

1. *Leave the men at home*

On the whole male partners have a tendency to dampen the joy of the experience, with phrases such as, 'Have you finished yet?' and 'Haven't we been in this shop three times already?' With a few exceptions, they also tend to be non-committal about which item of clothing suits you best, either opting for a 'Looks great, get that one' in a bid for a quick exit, or being too polite to point out that your butt looks the size of a small country in those skin-tight leggings. Girls-only is an absolute must.

2. Leave the kids at home

Dragging screaming and hungry kids or (worse) moaning teenagers from designer outlet to shoe shop is not conducive to sensible shopping. Like a nagging partner, impatient offspring will either lead you to pick up the nearest unsuitable garment without trying it on, or send you home empty-handed. And, unless your friend has also brought her brood, she's not going to be happy.

3. Decide where you need to go

Don't wait until you get there to discover that she needs to buy crockery and toys and you're after an outfit for a cocktail party. Discuss what you both need to get and try and choose a shopping centre that accommodates both of you.

4. Work out a plan

Wandering aimlessly around the mall and chatting is all very well, but you're likely to miss the shops you came for. Pinpoint stores you want to head to first and chat on the way.

> 'Neither a borrower, nor a lender be; for loan oft loses
> both itself and friend.'
>
> FROM *HAMLET* BY WILLIAM SHAKESPEARE
>
> (*c.*1564 –1616)

5. *Don't split up*

There's no point in arranging a two-pronged attack on the world of fashion if your partner in crime is not there when you need an opinion. Being stuck in a changing room with nothing but your indecision for company is the plight of the lone shopper, not you.

6. *Know your limits*

Some shopping buddies are more reckless than others, especially when you're the one spending the cash. Having shown them several possible outfits, they morph into the devil on your shoulder telling you to splash out and buy them all! Don't listen unless you can really afford it. Set yourself a spending limit and know exactly what it is you're after; if it's an outfit for a wedding you need, ignore those designer jeans.

> 'Whoever said money can't buy happiness simply didn't
> know where to go shopping.'
>
> BO DEREK, AMERICAN ACTRESS AND MODEL

7. Look for value

Instead of thinking of price alone, work out the cost-per-wear ratio before you part with your cash. To do this, divide the price by the number of times you are likely to wear the item. For instance, if a pair of boots costs £80 and you are likely to wear them three times a week for six months, the cost per wear is only £1.02 – and that's if you don't dig them out again next year. By the same token, a glittery silver dress that costs you £40 may only be worn three times, making a cost per wear of £13.33.

8. Honesty is the best policy

The biggest advantage of having your best mate on a shopping trip is that she will tell you exactly what she thinks. Give her the same courtesy. There's no point in telling her she looks great to spare her feelings. She won't thank you when she decides she looks ridiculous in her new outfit.

> 'Friends are born, not made.'
> HENRY ADAMS, US AUTHOR AND HISTORIAN
> (1838–1918)

9. Don't start with an empty stomach

A gorgeous lunch may be part of the whole experience, but if your stomach is rumbling by the time you reach the mall, you won't focus on anything else. And when it comes to choosing where to eat, you'll blow all the money you saved not buying that fourth top by ordering a big meal.

10. *Make it enjoyable*

Although scouring the stores for a great new look rates high on most women's idea of fun, it isn't everybody's cup of tea. If your friend has dragged you along reluctantly, try and enter the spirit of things and let her choose outfits for you to try on. You'll soon find the experience of shopping with a friend is infinitely more fun than you imagined – and it certainly beats doing it alone.

I'll Sign for You

Theologian and musician Albert Schweitzer was once approached by two women who asked if he was Albert Einstein (the two bore an uncanny resemblance). The Nobel Prizewinner replied graciously, 'I can quite understand your mistake, for he has the same kind of hair as I have. But inside, my head is altogether different. However, he is a very old friend of mine – would you like me to give you his autograph?' Which he duly did, signing it, 'Albert Einstein, by way of his friend, Albert Schweitzer'.

Snacks for Saints and Sinners

Gossiping, laughing, shopping and pampering can give a woman an appetite and no quality time at home with friends is complete without a few plates of nibbles. Each of the following comes with a saintly alternative, but feel free to let your devilish side win out.

SINFUL SKINS

INGREDIENTS:
- 6 medium baking potatoes
- 6 rashers of bacon (optional)
- Olive oil
- Rapeseed or vegetable oil
- Freshly ground pepper (optional)
- 110 g (4 oz) grated cheddar cheese
- 110 g (4 oz) sour cream

① Wash the potatoes, rub with olive oil and bake in the oven at 200 °C (390 °F or gas mark 6) for 45–50 minutes.

② Meanwhile, fry or grill the bacon on a medium to low heat for about 10 minutes, until crisp. Drain on paper towels and crumble or chop when cool.

③ When the potatoes are cooked let them cool for a few minutes, until you can handle them. Cut them in half and scoop the insides out with a spoon, leaving ½ cm (about ¼ inch) of potato on the skin. Reserve what you have scooped out for another use. (You can always have sausage and mash the following night.)

④ Turn the oven up to 230 °C (450 °F or gas mark 8) and brush the skins with the rapeseed or vegetable oil. Sprinkle with salt.

⑤ Place in a roasting tin and bake for 20 minutes, flipping the skins halfway through cooking time. Remove from oven and leave till cool enough to handle.

⑥ Fill the skins with the cheese and bacon and return to the oven for about 2 minutes, or until the cheese is bubbling.

⑦ Transfer to a serving plate and add a dollop of sour cream to each skin. Serves 4–6.

"Nearly eleven o'clock," said Pooh happily.
"You're just in time for a little smackerel of something."'
FROM *THE HOUSE AT POOH CORNER*,
BY A. A. MILNE (1882–1956)

NOT-SO-WICKED WEDGES

These make a great alternative to the Sinful Skins as they are only 1 per cent fat and just as delicious. Tuck in!

INGREDIENTS:

> 4 medium to large potatoes, scrubbed and cut into wedges
> Low-fat cooking spray
> Sea salt to taste
> 2–3 tablespoons fresh rosemary, chopped

① Spray a baking sheet with the cooking spray and arrange the wedges on the tray.

② Lightly spritz the potato wedges with more cooking spray until evenly coated.

③ Sprinkle generously with sea salt and chopped rosemary.

④ Bake in the oven at 200 °C (390 °F or gas mark 6) for 35–40 minutes, turning occasionally, until cooked through and golden.

⑤ Serve with low-fat crème fraiche with some snipped chives stirred through or a low-fat dip. Serves 4.

CHEESY OLIVE PARCELS

Naughty but very, very nice!

INGREDIENTS:
- 200 g (8 oz) finely grated sharp cheese, e.g. mature cheddar
- 100 g (4oz) butter, at room temperature
- 340 g (12 oz) pimiento green olives, pitted
- 100 g (4oz) flour

① Blend the cheese and butter thoroughly, then mix in the flour until a dough is formed.

② Roll out to ½ cm (¼ inch) thickness then cut into squares of about 5 cm (2 inches).

③ Place an olive into the centre of each square and wrap the dough around it, taking care to seal the ends.

④ Place on a greased baking tray and bake in the oven at 190 °C (375 °F or gas mark 5) for 15 minutes, or until golden brown. Serves 4.

BRUSCHETTA BE GOOD

This low-fat bruschetta has a delicious fresh taste – use the best quality olive oil you can find (and use less or more depending on how virtuous you feel).

INGREDIENTS:
- 8 slices Italian or French bread, about 1.5 cm (½ inch) thick
- 1 garlic clove
- 4 teaspoons olive oil
- 1 teaspoon salt
- 4 ripe tomatoes, chopped
- 2 tablespoons fresh basil, torn into small pieces

① Toast or grill the bread until light brown.

② Meanwhile peel and halve the garlic clove, then rub the cut sides over the top of the toasted bread.

③ Brush some oil over each slice and sprinkle with a little salt.

④ Top with the fresh tomato and sprinkle with plenty of basil. Serves 4.

'Money can't buy friends, but you can get a better class of enemy.'
SPIKE MILLIGAN, BRITISH COMEDIAN (1918–2002)

Fat is Infectious!

Choose your friends carefully – especially if you are prone to weight issues. *A New England Journal of Medicine* study, published in 2007, claimed that people can 'catch' obesity from their pals.

The theory is that you mirror the behaviour of your friends and, if they tend to overeat, you are subconsciously encouraged to do the same. The strange thing is, you don't even have to be with them. Even those who didn't live near their fat friends were more likely to be overweight themselves.

BAD AND BOOZY CHOCOLATE MUFFINS

Snacks don't get much more wicked than this! If the chocolate isn't enough to give a health freak apoplexy, a hint of brandy should do the trick. They are quick and easy to make and perfectly yummy to eat. You will need a muffin tray and eight paper cases.

INGREDIENTS:
  125 g (5 oz) good-quality plain chocolate
  75 g (3 oz) butter
  3 eggs
  60 g (2½ oz) icing sugar
  1 tablespoon (10g / ½ oz) self-raising flour
  1 tablespoon (15 ml) brandy (optional)

① Line the muffin tray with the paper cases.

② Break the chocolate into small chunks and melt in the microwave. Or place the chocolate in a Pyrex bowl and warm over a pan of hot water until all the lumps are gone, then remove from heat.

③ Cut the butter into small chunks and stir into the warm chocolate.

④ Break the eggs into a large bowl and whisk until fluffy and thick.

⑤ Fold in the sugar and flour and mix well, then add the chocolate mixture.

⑥ Add the brandy, if using, and stir well, then divide the mixture evenly between the paper cases.

⑦ Bake for 8 minutes in a very hot oven at 240 °C (575 °F or gas mark 9).

⑧ Cool on a wire rack and serve warm.

> 'The only reward of virtue is virtue; the only way to have a friend is to be one'
> RALPH WALDO EMERSON, POET, ESSAYIST
> AND PHILOSOPHER (1803–1882)

FAT-FREE FRUIT KEBABS

Fruit is so easy to eat this way that it makes great finger food, with none of the guilt of the above. You can vary the recipe and use any mixture of seasonal fruit that is firm enough to be skewered. You'll need 8–12 wooden skewers.

INGREDIENTS:
- 1 pineapple
- 1 melon (any variety)
- 1 punnet (250–400 g) strawberries
- 1 handful grapes
- 1 mango
- 200 ml (7 fl oz) low-fat vanilla yoghurt

① Using a long sharp knife, cut the pineapple into thick slices and remove the skin. Cut into large chunks, at least 3 cm (1 inch) wide.

② Cut the melon into similar-sized chunks then peel and chop the mango into chunks.

③ Wash and hull the strawberries then thread all the fruit onto the kebabs.

④ Serve with the vanilla yoghurt as a dip.

Love and Friendship

Love is like the wild rose-briar;
Friendship like the holly-tree.
The holly is dark when the rose-briar blooms,
But which will bloom most constantly?

The wild rose-briar is sweet in spring,
Its summer blossoms scent the air;
Yet wait till winter comes again,
And who will call the wild-briar fair?

Then scorn the silly rose-wreath now,
And deck thee with the holly's sheen,
That, when December blights thy brow,
He may still leave thy garland green.

EMILY BRONTË

Friends on Holiday

If you've passed the test of round-the-clock friendship and enjoy holidaying with your favourite ladies, why not think outside the box and try something a bit different this year? Instead of just soaking up the sun, why not add a different angle to your hols? Leave the dreary nine-to-five behind with these great getaway ideas.

CHILLING OUT IN THE COUNTRY

Sometimes all you really want with a good friend is the chance to sit and chat nineteen to the dozen without any distractions. The perfect solution: hire your very own country getaway where you can natter away over indulgent home-cooked dinners and during rambling walks with plenty of fresh air (helpful for burning off those big dinners!). There are lots of specialist websites where you can find a lovely cute cottage to rent for a week and if you gather together a group of close friends you can split the cost evenly. Then just load the car with your favourite vino, pasta and cheese and warm up your jaw muscles for a week of talking about life, the universe and everything.

DO GO IF:

You haven't had the chance to catch up properly with your oldest friends in absolutely ages. You'll have all the time you need to hear about everything that's going on with them, plus you can relive all those cringeworthy mistakes of your youth along the way! You'll laugh till you cry in front of a roaring fire as your friends remind you of old ugly perms and even uglier old boyfriends.

DON'T GO IF:

A friend has recently had a sad time of it. If she's been through a break-up or bereavement or lost her job, the last thing she'll want is too much time on her hands to sit around and brood. Keep her busy instead and take her on an eventful city break that will keep her mind on far happier things. Fill her time with theatre trips, museums, walking tours and, of course, plenty of cake, as any good friend would do.

> 'If I had to choose between betraying my country and betraying my friend, I hope I should have the guts to betray my country.'
> FROM *TWO CHEERS FOR DEMOCRACY*
> BY E. M. FORSTER (1879–1970)

CULTURE VULTURE

You can pick up great deals on flights and hotels to major cultural cities, so all that's left is to slip on some trusty comfortable shoes for plenty of exploring and make sure the camera is fully charged.

DO GO IF:

You both share a passion for history, travel and new experiences. Also, a big appetite helps: there's no point soaking up all that culture without sampling the local cuisine too. Just think of all the calories you'll burn walking round the museums . . .

DON'T GO IF:

Your best friend's idea of a perfect holiday is to lie by a pool and only move to reach for her Jackie Collins paperback or a Long Island Iced Tea. City breaks can be lovely and sunny but there's always lots going on and plenty to see. The last thing you want is to be dragging around a friend who really just wanted to veg out for a week and top up her tan.

Things Only Women Understand

The need for the same shoe in every colour.
Why shopping when you're in debt really does make sense.
Salad isn't only for rabbits.
Not having to explain your route in endless detail when arriving at a party.
Why 'you look fine' doesn't cut the mustard.
What a cat is thinking.
All bathroom scales are inaccurate.
Crying can be fun.
Eyelash curlers.
Other women.

FEELING HOT, HOT, HOT

For many of us, a classic beach holiday is the ideal way to unwind – and what better way to relax in the sunshine than with a really good friend? Lots of travel companies and websites rent out apartments close to the beach, some with their own private pool, where you can laze around in the midday sun, get a barbeque going and dig through a big bonkbuster novel. If you fly to the nearest city and then hire a car, even getting there will feel like a great road trip, driving on the wrong side of the road and trying out some languages you haven't used since school. Some wonderful destinations in Europe that offer culture and great food, as well as beautiful beaches, are the Italian island of Sardinia, the Catalonian coast in Spain and the Côte d'Azur in France (go during the Cannes Film Festival and you've got every chance of spotting a celebrity) but if it's exotic locations and adventure you're after, book tickets to the Far East where you can explore the breathtaking beaches of Thailand, Malaysia or Cambodia.

DO GO IF:

You can take the heat. Check the climate and humidity for the time of year before you're go and make sure that you're going to be able to cope with soaring summer temperatures. Wherever you decide to go, make sure you always carry water and sunscreen with you and stay in the shade or take a restorative nap at midday, when the sun is at its fiercest.

DON'T GO IF:

You think you might get on each other's nerves after a few solid days of being together (see 'The Danger Zone'). A lot of the time it'll be just the two of you so if someone's sulking after day three, it's not going to feel like a very relaxing break. Plan lots of activities to do together (like hiring scooters and exploring the local countryside or going on a snorkelling trip) but pack a few books and your iPod to keep you occupied when you need some time apart: why not try an audiobook to while away a few solitary hours?

Excuses, Excuses

Take a leaf out of Noël Coward's book when it comes to evading unwanted dinner engagements, and do it in style. When Coward was accosted and asked to dinner by a friend, he explained that he was unable to come, as he was leaving for Jamaica that evening. 'How lovely! When will you be back?' asked the friend, to which Coward replied, 'In the spring, with the swallows. You'll recognize me easily among them.'

Chick Lit

'Books and friends should be few but good.'
PROVERB

Book clubs are all the rage and they give great focus to an otherwise ordinary evening together. They also cost very little – the price of a book or a trip to your local library – and give you and your pals a great excuse to meet up for a good chinwag. Simply choose a book you all fancy reading and buy or borrow a copy each. Take everyone's busy lifestyle into account and make sure you leave enough time to finish the book. Arranging to meet once a month should be long enough. Write down points that occur to you as you are reading the book, and bring them up in the meeting. For example, is the heroine too demure and weak-willed, or a product of the age in which she lived? Examine the mistakes and behaviour of the main characters and discuss their relationships. It's amazing how a discussion about fictional characters can bring out peoples' real opinions on all sorts of subjects: you may learn a lot more about your friends than you thought.

SUGGESTED READS

The Divine Secrets of the Ya-Ya Sisterhood
Rebecca Wells
> A deeply moving account of the bond between four women from Tennessee, formed in childhood and lasting through-out their long lives.

Confessions of a Shopaholic
Sophie Kinsella

A light, fluffy and funny account of a wannabe fashion journalist and her struggle with her addiction to labels and ever-growing debt.

In the Company of the Courtesan
Sarah Dunant

A totally engaging novel, which has the rare quality of grabbing your attention while providing a history lesson. Set in Venice, it covers the career of a celebrated courtesan who has fled from the sacking of Rome in 1527. Told through the eyes of her constant companion, a loyal dwarf, it is occasionally racy but utterly enchanting.

'It is more fun to talk with someone who doesn't use long, difficult words but rather short, easy words like "What about lunch?"'
WINNIE THE POOH, FROM *POOH'S LITTLE BOOK OF INSTRUCTIONS*, INSPIRED BY A. A. MILNE (1882–1956)

Closure
Sarah Harris

> An ambitious radio presenter develops an obsession with a lifestyle guru, which leads her to correct past mistakes by cutting people out of her life. Witty and thought-provoking.

The Missing Person's Guide to Love
Susanna Jones

> Essentially a detective story, which follows distraught heroine Isabel as she searches for her missing friend, Julia. A beautifully written and compelling drama.

Emma
Jane Austen

> One of Austen's most famous heroines, Emma dreams of nothing but romance and matchmaking but can't spot real love, even when it's right under her perfectly pert little nose.

Twilight
Stephenie Meyer

> A vampire saga with a difference, the first book in this internationally best-selling series follows teenager Bella and her romance with a perfect boy – who just happens to be a vampire. A captivating read – definitely not just for teenagers.

The Poisonwood Bible
Barbara Kingsolver

An interesting and informative tale about a missionary family who move from Georgia to the Belgian Congo in 1959. Told through the eyes of five women – the mother and her four daughters – their tale mirrors the turmoil of the country in the post-colonial era.

Other Book Club Favourites

The White Tiger ....by Aravind Adiga
Notes on a Scandal ....by Zoë Heller
A Thousand Splendid Suns ....by Khaled Hosseini
*The Curious Incident of the Dog in the
Night-Time* ....by Mark Haddon
The Time Traveller's Wife ....by Audrey Niffenegger
We Need to Talk about Kevin ....by Lionel Shriver
The New Confessions ....by William Boyd
Enduring Love ....by Ian McEwan
The Lovely Bones ....by Alice Sebold
White Teeth ....by Zadie Smith
Wuthering Heights ....by Emily Brontë

The Golden Rules of Friendship

1. DON'T BE IRRITABLE

No matter how close you are, there will be times when some aspects of your friend's behaviour will annoy you. Chances are she feels the same way about you occasionally, but before you snap at her and start a full-scale row, force yourself to look at the bigger picture. Whoever is in the wrong, imagine your life without her before you speak. If your relationship is solid, that miserable thought should be enough to make you bite your tongue.

2. KEEP IT CALM

If you are about to lose your cool, and an argument is on the blink of erupting, make an excuse and walk away. When the heat has gone out of the situation, talk to her calmly about what was bugging you and, if you think she is doing something that will harm your friendship, tell her exactly how you feel.

3. BE LOYAL

Whatever others may say about her behind her back, make sure you stick up for her. It may take courage to stand up to her critics, but wouldn't you expect her to do the same for you? Knowing you can always count on someone to stick up for you, even when you're not there, is worth its weight in gold.

> 'Do not save your loving speeches
> For your friends till they are dead;
> Do not write them on their tombstones,
> Speak them rather now instead.'
> ANNA CUMMINS, AMERICAN POET
> AND EDUCATIONALIST

4. BE SUPPORTIVE

Life is full of huge decisions and your friend will turn to you for advice and comfort while she makes them. Listen to her opinion and give your advice, but remember to keep it objective. Make sure your advice isn't selfish. For example, if she wants to study abroad, or leave the company that you both work at, make sure your advice is not based on your desire for her to stay. Give her your opinion, but help her make the choice that is best for her, not for you.

A Supporting Role

Salma Hayek and *Bandidas* co-star Penélope Cruz have been best buddies for years and have watched each other's careers and lives blossom. But far from seeing themselves as rivals, they celebrate every triumph together.

After Penélope's Oscar nomination for *Vicky Cristina Barcelona* in January 2009, the delighted Salma threw a party at her lavish home in the Hollywood Hills.

The *Ugly Betty* star chose a *Vicky Cristina Barcelona* theme for the party and decked out her house with numerous photos of her best mate.

---

5. NEVER FLIRT WITH HER PARTNER

Be civil, be friendly, but never give her any cause for jealousy. More great friendships have been broken by the green-eyed monster than for any other reason. Even if you happen to have been friends with him long before they met, avoid in-jokes and anything that will exclude her or make her feel undermined. Likewise, you may think he's the biggest creep on earth but there is no surer way of losing a pal than to put the knife into her boyfriend or husband. If he is treating her badly, let her know you don't agree with his actions, but don't go calling him all the names under the sun – she will inevitably end up defending him.

6. RESPECT HER FAMILY

Your friend has every right to have a good moan about her mum, dad, brothers and sisters, but that doesn't mean you can. If you weigh in she's more likely to take their side and then, when the row has blown over, she'll resent the things you said about them. When you are around her relations, be polite and respectful and never let on you know any of the family secrets.

> 'Fate chooses our relatives, we choose our friends.'
> JACQUES DELILLE, FRENCH POET (1738–1813)

7. BE DISCREET

When a friend asks you not to tell a soul, make sure you listen. Gossiping can be tempting, but it is bound to come back and bite you, even if you just tell one person. A true friend can keep a secret to the grave and will be loved all the more for it.

8. DON'T EMBARRASS HER

Even those of us with a sense of humour would rather not hear some of the stories our mates drag up from time to time. If you know your friend is uncomfortable about some of the jokes you make at her expense, stop. A little gentle teasing is all well and good, but you need to know when she is getting upset. Remember to tailor your conversation to whoever you are with. When you're with her family, for example, keep your wilder stories to yourself.

Sharp-Witted Friends

Being able to tease one's friends and enjoy playful badinage is all part and parcel of friendship, as the following anecdote illustrates. Eminent playwright George Bernard Shaw once sent his friend, Winston Churchill, a couple of tickets for the first night of his play, *St Joan*, together with a little note saying, 'One for yourself, the other for a friend – if you have one.' Regrettably, Churchill couldn't make it on the night, so he sent Shaw a note explaining that he was otherwise engaged but that he would like tickets for the second night – 'if there is one'.

9. LEARN TO SAY SORRY

As the lovely Elton John once said, 'Sorry seems to be the hardest word', and many a great relationship has ended out of sheer stubbornness. After a heated exchange, you may feel you're totally right but, whether it takes a week, a month or a year, you will eventually realize that it doesn't matter. Losing a friend because you were too proud to say sorry is what will stick with you.

10. LAUGH IT OFF

The crucial ingredient in any steadfast and rewarding friendship is a shared sense of humour, and it can often be the means of overcoming all sorts of hurdles and challenges in your friendship. If your difference of opinion is one that can't be resolved you'll just have to laugh it off and agree to disagree. In fact, the moment when you both realize how ridiculous an argument has become can instantly bridge the divide and have you both crying with laughter and leaning on one another for support.

'It is easier to forgive an enemy than to forgive a friend.'
WILLIAM BLAKE, ENGLISH POET AND
ILLUSTRATOR (1757–1827)

Mad, Bad and Dangerous to Know

'Blessed are our enemies, for they tell us the
truth when our friends flatter us.'
ANONYMOUS

There are many touching tales of friendship in the Hollywood
archives but not all female bonding is a good thing. Here are a
few partnerships which fall into the category 'with friends like
these, who needs enemies'.

THELMA AND LOUISE (1991)

A weekend break turns into a crime spree and friends become
fugitives. Downtrodden housewife Thelma (played by Geena
Davis) and fast-food waitress Louise (Susan Sarandon) break
out of their mundane lives for a road trip but end up being
chased across the country after Louise shoots a man who tries
to rape Thelma.

MEMORABLE LINE:
Thelma: 'You said you 'n' me was gonna get out of
town and for once just really let our hair down. Well,
darlin', look out 'cause my hair is comin' down!'

ALL ABOUT EVE (1950)

Bette Davis stars in this classic about a Broadway star and an ingénue. Fervent fan Eve Harrington (played by Anne Baxter) wheedles her way into the life of her idol, Margo Channing (Davis), by becoming a secretary and confidante. Before long she is taking over her life, flirting with Margo's man and even stealing the lead roles from under her nose.

MEMORABLE LINE:
>   Margo: 'Fasten your seatbelts, it's going to be a bumpy night!'

'In the end, we will remember not the words of our enemies, but the silence of our friends.'
MARTIN LUTHER KING JR, CIVIL RIGHTS
MOVEMENT LEADER (1929–1968)

SINGLE WHITE FEMALE (1992)

This movie is enough to put you off flat-sharing for life. Software designer Allie Jones (Bridget Fonda) puts an ad for a flatmate in the paper after splitting with her boyfriend. Hedy Carlson (Jennifer Jason Leigh) seems the ideal roomie at first but, as the two women get to know each other, her behaviour becomes increasingly weird. She erases Allie's messages from her ex, copies her clothes and even gets her hair cut exactly the same way. When Allie is reconciled with her ex, Hedy's strange behaviour turns psychotic.

MEMORABLE LINE:
Allie: 'I know you weren't yourself when you did this, Hedy.'
Hedy: 'I know. I was *you*.'

Revolutionary Friends

Colombian novelist Gabriel García Márquez is said to have been a great friend of Cuba's Fidel Castro, who was a great admirer of the writer's novels – so much so, in fact, that when Márquez won the Nobel Prize for Literature in 1982, Castro sent 1,500 bottles of Cuban rum to Stockholm where Márquez received the award.

HEATHERS (1989)

The Heathers are three trendy but bitchy schoolgirls who make up the hub of a social clique. When they set their sights on Veronica (played by Winona Rider) to become part of their group, she is dragged into their bullying and mental torture of fellow pupils. But she pulls away after falling for rebel JD, played by Christian Slater, and suddenly the Heathers begin to die, one by one . . .

MEMORABLE LINE:
Heather Chandler: 'Grow up, Heather. Bulimia's so '87.'

Girls' Night In

What better way to spend an evening than curling up on the sofa with your closest pals, a bottle of wine and some snacks? Nights in give you a chance for a proper catch-up with no interruptions and a chance to share those 'for your ears only' stories. But why not introduce a different element to the classic night in?

STYLE SWAP

We all have clothes lurking at the back of the wardrobe that were a bad buy, made us look dumpy or simply don't fit any more. It doesn't mean they have to be consigned to the scrap heap. Instead, host a fashion-swapping party: they are huge fun and you might even finish up with a whole new wardrobe.

① Set a date with your friends for a few weeks' time, leaving them enough time to have a thoroughly good rummage in the forgotten corners of their wardrobes.

② Be ruthless. If you have a new pair of jeans you've been meaning to slim into for two years, bung them on the party pile. Let's face it, they'll only take up space in the closet for another two years! And don't forget those neglected shoes, bags and other accessories.

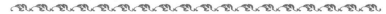

③ Buy some sheets of coloured paper, in three or four different shades, and cut into small squares, large enough to write your friends' names on.

④ On the night, clear a space in your living room for three or four piles of clothes – e.g. tops, skirts and trousers, dresses and accessories – and give each pile a colour, corresponding with your paper slips. For example, skirts are in the blue pile, tops in the yellow pile, etc.

⑤ As each guest arrives, get her to sort her contributions into the piles. For each item added, write her name on a paper slip of the appropriate colour and put it into a large bowl. For example, if you put a skirt into the blue pile, a blue slip with your name on it goes into the bowl.

⑥ When everyone has divided up their contributions and is settled with a nice glass of wine and something to nibble on, pick out a coloured slip and read out the name. The named guest then gets to choose from the appropriate coloured pile. Read out each slip in turn until everyone has chosen their items.

⑦ If one or two guests have clothes that others particularly wanted, they can negotiate between themselves. At the end of the party, there are likely to be some items that, unfortunately, nobody wants. These can be bagged up to take to charity shop.

Famous Friendships

Dr Johnson and James Boswell
Charlotte Brontë and Elizabeth Gaskell
Ernest Hemingway and F. Scott Fitzgerald
Sir Edmund Hillary and Sherpa Tenzing
Bonnie and Clyde
Abbott and Costello
Butch Cassidy and the Sundance Kid
Jean-Paul Sartre and Simone de Beauvoir
David Niven and Errol Flynn
Laurel and Hardy

GAMES NIGHT

Organized games can liven up any gathering, whether it's just the two of you or a whole crowd. You can make things more fun by awarding small prizes to the winner of each game.

Small groups

If two or three of you are spending the evening together, a pack of cards may be all you need for a games night. Even the silliest games, such as Snap, Beggar my Neighbour and Pairs, are great fun with friends. Others that are great for small groups are Racing Demon, Rummy and Pick-up-Two. (The rules for all of these games are readily available on the Internet.)

But if you don't fancy cards, here are a few other fun games that can be played in a small gathering.

Six Degrees of Separation

This requires quite a lot of film and TV knowledge so it's a great one for movie-goers. One player suggests two random actors and the person to their left then has to connect them in six or fewer steps. You can use either films they have starred in together, or personal connections. For example, the six degrees between Brad Pitt and Nicole Kidman could be as follows:

Brad Pitt was in *Thelma and Louise* with Uma Thurman.
Uma Thurman was in *My Super-Ex Girlfriend* with Luke Wilson.
Luke Wilson is Owen Wilson's brother.
Owen Wilson was a voice in *Cars* with Paul Newman.
Paul Newman starred with Tom Cruise in *The Color of Money*.
Tom Cruise starred in *Days of Thunder* with Nicole Kidman.

Celebrity Twenty Questions

One player picks a well-known person, past or present, and the other players have twenty questions in which to guess who it is. 'Yes' and 'no' are the only permitted answers, so questions such as 'How old are you?' will be pointless. Whoever guesses the celebrity then takes the next turn.

Truth or Dare

Want to find out if your best mate really did snog your boss at the firm's Christmas party? Suggest a game of good old-fashioned Truth or Dare and start spinning. When the top of the bottle faces you, the player on your left will say 'truth or dare?' Choose truth and you must give an honest answer to any question she asks. Choose dare and you are up for a forfeit.

> 'Some people come into our lives and quickly go.
> Some stay for a while and leave footprints on our hearts.
> And we are never, ever the same.'
> ANONYMOUS

LARGER GROUPS

Soul Search

This is a great ice-breaker if you have a large group who don't know each other well. Every question starts with 'I'm searching for . . .' and with each scenario those who think they are the correct person put their hand up. For example, 'I'm searching for the person who has the newest car' might mean several people raise their hand and the real winner gets a point. Those who raise their hand incorrectly lose a point each.

You kick off and the person who fits the bill asks the next question.

Other examples include: the person with the most handbags, the oldest person here, the first person to show me a family photo or the person who has travelled the most in the last two years. They can be tailored to fit your own group and can be as saucy or as clean as you like. The winner is the person with the most points.

> 'Mighty proud I am that I am able to have a spare bed
> for my friends.'
> SAMUEL PEPYS, DIARIST, MP AND NAVAL
> ADMINISTRATOR (1633–1703)

I Have Never . . .

Remember this one? It can be played in groups of four or more and you can either play it as a drinking game or a game where pennies or counters are given each time. It also works well around a dinner table.

Each person takes it in turn to announce something they have never done. For example, 'I have never been to Italy' or 'I have never read a Jane Austen novel'.

Everybody who *has* done the activity in question then has to take a drink (if you are playing it as a drinking game) or receive a counter.

Establish how many times you will go round the table and, at the end, the person with the most tokens (if playing this way) is the winner. If you're playing the drinking version, the losers will know who they are by the end of the night!

Who Needs Romance?

Burlesque dancer Dita Von Teese is used to having men lusting after her but finding herself single in 2009, she arranged a special Valentine's Day get-together for the girls. She and her close friends booked a weekend in Paris, the city of love, and made a date with some fabulously fattening cakes.

'I have organized an afternoon Valentine's tea with all my girlfriends at a hotel in Paris. They are all flying in and we will have tea and fabulous pastries,' she said, before leaving for her alternative Valentine's trip.

You're Not Going to Like This, But . . .

'The best way to keep your friends is
not to give them away.'
WILSON MIZNER, AMERICAN DRAMATIST (1876–1933)

Once in a while we all have to broach difficult topics. Perhaps you have to tell her you are moving away, or that you have heard malicious gossip about her from someone she confided in. It could be that you want to confront her about her bad behaviour, or that of her partner or husband. It's bound to be painful, but damage limitation is the key.

PICK YOUR LOCATION

If your conversation is likely to result in one or both of you getting upset or angry, then don't bring it up in a crowded restaurant or a very public place. Suggest a night in or a chat over a cup of coffee or, better still, go for a walk. Not having to make eye contact as you talk can actually be helpful when difficult issues are being brought out into the open, and walking and talking at the same time tends to help the conversation flow.

TIMING IS EVERYTHING

Make sure she is in the best frame of mind to hear your news and wait for the appropriate moment. Don't come bursting through the door and blurt it out before she has had a chance to say 'hello'. Chat a little first and try to steer the conversation round to the topic on your mind. If she is already stressed or upset about anything else, hold fire for another time.

CHOOSE YOUR WORDS CAREFULLY

Try and put it as tactfully as you can and listen to what she says in return. Watch her body language to gauge the effect of your conversation on her and don't get defensive if she takes it badly.

> 'Think where man's glory most begins and ends,
> And say my glory was I had such friends.'
> FROM 'THE MUNICIPAL GALLERY REVISITED'
> BY W. B. YEATS (1865–1939)

BE PREPARED FOR THE FALLOUT

You may be anticipating a reaction but stay calm if it is worse than expected. She was unprepared and so can't control her emotional response as well as you, so make sure you are ready to take it on the chin – as long as it is only figuratively!

Critical Friends

Nineteenth-century art critic John Ruskin was always at pains to point out that even if he gave a terrible review about an artist's work, it shouldn't affect his friendship with that artist. However, the artists themselves weren't quite so eager to agree with Ruskin. 'Next time I meet you I shall knock you down,' one such friend reportedly said, 'but I trust it will make no difference to our friendship.'

After the Storm

'Forsake not an old friend; for the new is not
comparable to him; a new friend is a new wine;
when it is old, thou shalt drink it with pleasure.'
THE BIBLE, ECCLESIASTICUS, CH. 9, V. 10

Arguments are inevitable in any relationship but it needn't be
the end. Learning to get past disagreement is the key to keeping
your friendship on track.

GIVE HER SPACE

Time is a great healer, as they say, and it also allows hot heads
to cool down. Don't hang around after a blazing row, or you
may be tempted to put the boot in one last time. Walk away
and leave it until the next day when tempers won't be so raw.

EAT HUMBLE PIE

Pride comes before a fallout but, unless you swallow it pretty
soon afterwards, it will cause an irreparable rift. You may think
you are in the right but an apology is the first step to fixing the
problem; chances are she will apologize as soon as you do and
all will be well again.

FORGIVE OR FORGET

Most of the issues that cause tempers to flare are relatively minor, and pretty forgivable. So unless she has murdered your mother, try and find it in your heart to forgive and, if you can't, put it to the back of your mind and agree to disagree.

LET IT GO

Once an issue is dealt with, try not to revisit the argument by bringing it up again. You now know her opinion doesn't match yours so returning to a difficult subject can only make matters worse.

> 'It is great to have friends when one is young, but indeed it is still more so when you are getting old. When we are young, friends are, like everything else, a matter of course. In the old days we know what it means to have them.'
>
> EDVARD GRIEG, NORWEGIAN COMPOSER (1843–1907)

Shifting Sands

'Don't walk in front of me, I may not follow.
Don't walk behind me, I may not lead.
Walk beside me and be my friend.'
ALBERT CAMUS, FRENCH AUTHOR AND
PHILOSOPHER (1913–1960)

It takes the strongest of bonds to survive the test of time and the changing circumstances that life throws at you. You can never guarantee that your lives will move at the same pace, and you will need to work at the relationship if you don't want to be left behind. Work, romance and children all have the effect of pushing friends further down the list of priorities and that can be a tough pill to swallow.

LEAVING SCHOOL

Having spent every day together for five years or more, leaving school can come as a shock. Whether you go to university or get a job, it is at this point that your lives begin to take separate paths. If further education is involved it may mean a geographical distance between you, but even a different choice of career can distance you emotionally. At work and uni there are new challenges, different lifestyles and, more importantly, new friends. Everyone changes in the first few years after school and growing up can mean growing apart.

Of course, you will meet new friends but that doesn't mean you can't put in the effort to be with your best pal. If you are still in the same area, keep one night each week free to meet up and do your best to keep that sacred.

For those who are separated by geographical distance, out of sight should never be out of mind. Make regular emails a must, even if it's just sending a joke, call once a week and try and visit when you can.

> 'The most beautiful discovery true friends make is that they can grow separately without growing apart.'
> KATHERINE MANSFIELD, AUTHOR (1888–1923)

OTHER HALVES

When a relationship gets more serious, and your friend looks ready to settle down for life, you may need to learn to take a step back. Though she will still value you, she is more likely to put her partner's wishes before yours. Respect that and work round it. If you're the first to find your soulmate, be considerate of her feelings and make sure you find time for her.

A great way of making sure you don't drift apart is arranging a weekly class or activity. Join a salsa club, a gym or a computer course and spend an extra hour or so together afterwards. The benefit of a weekly routine is that you're less likely to pull out or let other things get in the way.

If you can't meet in the evenings as often as you would like, spend time together at weekends, shopping or meeting for lunch. If you're lucky enough to have partners that get on, include them in some of your plans, but make sure you still get some time together without them.

Ten Reasons Why a Friend is Better Than a Husband

- she wants you to go out and he wants you to stay in
- you don't mind if she goes out with another woman
- she never drops her dirty clothes on your floor
- you can show her the *fabulous* shoes you bought without hearing, 'How much?'
- she never moans about your cooking
- you can tell her anything, no matter how embarrassing
- she'll never tell you off for your bad behaviour – no matter how embarrassing
- he'll never give you a straight answer
- she'll tell the truth – whether you want to hear it or not
- you can moan about your husband when you're with her!

CHILDREN

Nothing will dominate your friend's waking hours and love as completely as a new baby, but at the same time, this is when she will most need your support. You may find that the only way to see her as often as you'd like is to get involved. Pop round when she's on her own with the baby and help her out if she needs a break. Offer to take the tot out for a walk in the pram while she has a shower, or babysit while she and her husband go out. She'll appreciate what a wonderful friend you are and the support will be vital. When things calm down and she gets a semblance of her life back, she'll be up for the occasional night out and will relish it more than ever.

WORK COMMITMENTS

Your lives are bound to take different paths and while one of you lands a high-flying, high-stress job, it's possible that the other may be at home with children, or working part-time. A stark contrast in lifestyles shouldn't mean a change in your relationship. Remember, the grass is always greener on the other side so don't envy or resent her choices. Applaud her achievements, no matter how different they are to yours, and encourage her when times are tough. Again, a weekly meet at an exercise class, or a regular lunch date, means you will always stay in touch.

'Anybody can sympathize with the sufferings of a friend, but it requires a very fine nature to sympathize with a friend's success.'
OSCAR WILDE, NOVELIST, PLAYWRIGHT
AND WIT (1854–1900)

MOVING AWAY

Being divided by a vast distance is the toughest thing for any friendship. You're used to popping round to see your friend and sharing all your social events with her and, if one of you has moved away, it can leave a big void in your life. Some long-distance friendships gradually fade away but that needn't be the case. It takes work and commitment, but modern technology means you can keep in touch so much easier these days.

RETIREMENT

If your lifelong friendship makes it to this milestone, congratulations! You know each other inside out and share a lot of interests. Many retirees find that the biggest change is going from being too busy to having too much time on their hands, so thank goodness you have each other. Now is the time to enjoy all the things you said you'd do together and never got round to – even if that includes parachute jumping and swimming the English Channel. Go for it!

In Memoriam

Three friends had just attended the funeral of one of their colleagues and they were all touched by the ceremony. They began to speculate about their own funerals and the first one said: 'When I die, I'd like people to look at me in the coffin and say "Wow, she sure looks good for her age." '

The second friend said, 'I'd like them to look at me and say "She was a really kind person and a truly good friend." '

The third one said, 'I'd like them to look at me and say "Look! She's breathing!" '

Girls' Night Out

If you always end up going to the same pub, club or restaurant you could be getting into a social rut. So next time you are planning a night out, throw in a few of these alternatives and liven things up!

> 'If you are single there is always one thing you should take out with you on a Saturday night . . . your friends.'
> **CARRIE BRADSHAW, FROM THE TV SERIES**
> *SEX AND THE CITY*

SPICE IT UP

Latin American dance clubs are all the rage and many host salsa nights, where guests receive an hour's salsa lesson before the real dancing begins. Look on the Internet for your local venues, then dust off your best glittery outfit and get moving!

BOOGIE ON THE BUS

If there is a huge crowd of you, why not try a party bus. These are run by private companies who will drive you to several venues, while you carry on partying in-between. They are not hugely expensive (unless you want to include dinner in the deal) and save you having to get taxis all over town, but many have a minimum number for bookings.

Pre-Party Songs

'Man, I Feel Like a Woman!' ....Shania Twain
'Get the Party Started'...Pink
'Dancing Queen'..Abba
'I Don't Feel Like Dancing'........................Scissor Sisters
'Girls Just Wanna Have Fun'.....................Cyndi Lauper
'Hips Don't Lie' ....Shakira
'Here Come the Girls' ....Ernie K. Doe
'Showing Out' ....Mel and Kim
'Don't Cha' ....Pussycat Dolls
'Get into the Groove'...Madonna

BACK TO SCHOOL

Not for the faint-hearted. Get your gym slip out and put your hair in pigtails for a return to the best days of your life. 'School disco' theme nights now run in nightclubs and other venues in many towns and cities. Look up the next one closest to you on the Internet, and bring back those heady days of youth!

Schoolboy Chums

When at studying at Harrow School, would-be poet Lord Byron was great friends with Robert Peel. One day, seeing Peel about to get beaten by a senior boy at the school, Byron, who had no hope of fighting the older boy off incapacitated as he was by his club foot, instead demanded to know how many stripes the boy was going to inflict upon his poor friend. 'What's that to you?' asked the senior boy angrily. 'Because', replied Byron, his voice shaking with anger, 'I would take half.'

LEARN YOUR LESSON

Night classes are not all about flower arranging and don't always take place in colleges. From pole dancing and belly dancing to cookery and crystal healing, there has to be a course for you. And if you want to make it to one, scour the Internet for evening events such as cheese and wine talks and Viking cuisine nights (they really do exist!).

'Lots of people want to ride with you in the limo.
But what you want is someone who will take the bus with you
when the limo breaks down.'
OPRAH WINFREY, AMERICAN TALK-SHOW HOST

BOWLED OVER

Tenpin bowling has to be one of the most entertaining group events invented. Not only can you do it at any age, but it requires a minimum level of fitness and won't disgrace the unfit. Make sure you book an alley in advance to avoid disappointment and think carefully about what to wear. Never ever wear a miniskirt and, if the outfit only looks good with high heels, forget it – bowling shoes are no substitute for Jimmy Choos!

Thorny Questions

Do you fancy my boyfriend/partner/husband?

DO SAY: I think he's lovely but he's not my type.

DON'T SAY: I think he's gorgeous. If you hadn't got there first, I'd have been in there like a shot.

Do I look fat in this dress?

DO SAY: You never look fat in anything but that's not as flattering as it could be.

DON'T SAY: That reminds me, I found this great new diet in my magazine.

Did everyone know how drunk I was last night?

DO SAY: We were all in the same boat and you were no worse than the others . . .

DON'T SAY: You were minging. Do you want to see the photos?

What do you think of my new haircut? I'm not sure it suits me . . .

DO SAY: It's great, but I think it will look even better in a couple of weeks.

DON'T SAY: Oh my God! I'd sue!

The Changing Tastes of Women

WHAT TO DRINK ON A NIGHT OUT

Aged 18 – alcopops
Aged 28 – white wine
Aged 38 – red wine
Aged 48 – champagne
Aged 58 – sherry
Aged 68 – hot toddy

WHAT MAKES A GREAT DATE

Aged 18 – cinema and burger
Aged 28 – a free meal
Aged 38 – a diamond
Aged 48 – a bigger diamond
Aged 58 – going back to his place
Aged 68 – going home alone

THE IDEAL MAN

Aged 18 – tall, dark and handsome
Aged 28 – tall, dark and handsome with money
Aged 38 – tall, dark, handsome and unmarried
Aged 48 – tall, male and in possession of his own hair
Aged 58 – male and in possession of his own teeth
Aged 68 – male

FAVOURITE PASTIME

Aged 18 – shopping
Aged 28 – shopping
Aged 38 – shopping
Aged 48 – shopping
Aged 58 – shopping
Aged 68 – shopping

'Who finds a faithful friend, finds a treasure.'
JEWISH PROVERB

Friends Together Again

FLYING VISIT

A Somerset woman overcame her fear of flying and travelled three thousand miles to see a friend she met seventy years before.

Theta House was seventy-five when she plucked up the courage to get on a plane to Canada, where her childhood pal, Jean Gowe, was living.

The two girls became firm friends when Jean was evacuated to Frome from Hastings at the age of six. She moved in with seven-year-old Theta and her guardians, and the pair were soon up to mischief. 'We were always going off for adventures on our own,' Theta told the *Somerset Guardian* newspaper. 'Sometimes we'd climb the apple trees and hide the apples in our clothes and then sneak them up to our bedroom – even though we knew we weren't allowed. We had a lot of fun together.'

Sadly, the women lost touch after Jean emigrated to Canada at the age of seventeen, but a chance meeting with her brother, who was living in Frome, put Theta on the trail. The pair exchanged letters and in September 2008, Theta decided it was time they got together.

'I lost my husband, Hubert, five years ago, and have a fear of flying, but I knew I had to go,' she said. 'I really wanted to see Jean and didn't know whether I'd get the chance again.'

The intervening years melted away as the two friends caught up.

'We didn't stop chatting the whole time we were together,' she said. 'It was like the old days and I'm so proud of myself for going and really pleased I did.'

THANKS FOR THE MEMORIES

The website Friends Reunited was a lifesaver to one motorcyclist. Kevin, aged twenty-four, had a bad accident in 2002 and suffered partial memory loss as a result. Through the website he contacted his old school friends who helped him piece together his past life and came up with photos and memories from his schooldays.

FROM ENEMY TO ALLY

Dan Cherry and Nguyen Hong My were mortal enemies during the Vietnam War, when they went head to head in a fierce dogfight, but met again under very different circumstances nearly four decades later. Over the intervening years Cherry wondered what happened to the plane he shot down and whether the pilot survived and he finally got the opportunity to find out via a Vietnamese reality TV show that reunites people.

Though it was a bloody war that brought their lives together, their shared experience allowed them to develop a close bond – even paying visits to each other's homes in Vietnam and the US.

Cherry told the *Airforce Times* that their friendship holds an inspirational message for everyone: 'We think there is a real life lesson here for everyone, not just the military, not just aviators. Holding grudges doesn't do anybody any good.'

> 'We can live without religion and meditation, but we cannot survive without human affection.'
> **THE DALAI LAMA**

FARM FRIENDS

Former British land girls Evaline Bird and Vera Solomon were reunited after sixty years, only to discover they lived a mile apart. During the Second World War, the ladies had become close while working for the Land Army, the body of young girls drafted in to farms to replace the male workers.

The teenagers toiled in the fields of North Devon for a gruelling ten hours a day and lived together at night but, when the war ended and the soldiers returned to their old jobs, the Land Army was disbanded. Evaline and Vera moved to different towns and lost touch.

In the 1960s, Evaline and her husband Cyril moved to Paignton, South Devon, and Vera moved to the same town five years later.

It was not until 9 December 2008, however, that the ladies were reintroduced at an award ceremony at the town's Oldway Mansion. In recognition of their Land Army work, they were presented with a specially designed commemorative badge but went home with a whole lot more.

'This is a lovely Christmas present,' said Vera. 'We've got a lot to catch up on. We could never have imagined we lived so close after all these years. A lot of time has passed. We may have even seen each other in the town lots of times without even realizing who it was.'

Evaline was equally excited to be reunited with her old friend.

'It was lovely. It's a shame we didn't stay in touch but we'll certainly make up for lost time, which is fantastic.'

> 'True friends stab you in the front.'
> OSCAR WILDE, NOVELIST, PLAYWRIGHT
> AND WIT (1854–1900)

THE TELEGRAM BOYS

Former telegram delivery boys Ron Hart, Alex Boothroyd and Davey Hughes went their separate ways in 1947 when they were enrolled for National Service. They first met when they started work during the Second World War in a post office in Merseyside, most of them then aged just fourteen. Their job was often a gruelling one, as many of the telegrams they delivered carried MOD news of casualties at the front to distraught mothers and wives back home. There were about three hundred telegram boys at the time, so numerous were deliveries in the Merseyside area.

Mr Boothroyd organized a telegram-boy reunion in early 2009 when he learned that another former colleague, Ron Hart, lived in the area and they then got in touch with Davey Hughes. The three friends, now in their seventies and eighties, then gathered together to relive some old memories and share some jokes over a pint or two.

Ron summed it up when he said, 'We're very fortunate to be in touch with each other, sixty-three years after we worked together as children. It's fabulous!'

Auld Lang Syne

Should auld acquaintance be forgot,
And never brought to mind?
Should auld acquaintance be forgot,
And auld lang syne?
For auld lang syne, my dear,
For auld lang syne,
We'll tak a cup o' kindness yet,
For auld lang syne.

FROM 'AULD LANG SYNE' BY ROBERT BURNS

Techno Friends

One of the best things about living in this super-technological age is that it's created so many ways to stay in touch with friends, wherever and whoever you are. With a few clicks of a mouse and a 'hilarious' username you can link up to your Aunt Doris, your best friend from nursery or an old pal who now lives in Canada. Though it's always great to stay in touch, there are a few safeguards you should put into place when joining online communities and networking sites: always adjust security settings to make sure your personal information is only seen by your friends. Think about who's going to see your profile and any photos or blogs you're sharing – if your boss is on Facebook too, will he want to know that you spent the best part of Thursday morning thinking about what to have for lunch? And don't forget that cyber communications will never be as good as the real thing – don't get so friendly with your PC that your actual friends start to forget you!

EMAIL

Email is the grandfather of electronic messaging. It's great to be able to nip into an Internet cafe while on holiday and drop a quick message to your friends, letting them all know what you've been up to, saving you five separate phone calls. However, like a grandfather, emails can sometimes go on and on a bit and lose their train of thought, as it's so easy to ramble. Remember to keep things short and sweet in an email, especially as some friends might be wading through tonnes of them at work. And if you're catching up and asking questions of a friend, stick to two or three. Answering a whole list of back-and-forth questions can seem more like a chore than catching up.

> 'I can trust my friends. These people force me to examine, encourage me to grow.'
> CHER, AMERICAN SINGER AND ACTRESS

FRIENDS REUNITED

Friends Reunited took off in 2000 and quickly had long-lost friends from the first year of secondary school meeting up again to see how they'd all grown up. If you sign up, make sure you register each school you were at (they have lists by region, if you can't quite remember that far back!) and the years you attended that school so the website can link you to all the other users who attended the same school in the same year. You can also register which colleges and universities you went to, as well as old jobs. But make sure you have a careful think back before agreeing to any school reunion get-togethers: is there perhaps a reason you didn't stay friends with some of your old classmates?

Friends on the Line

Stephen Fry and Emma Thompson have been close friends since meeting at Cambridge and have continued their friendship through the years, even combining their shared strong wit and keen intellect on TV shows and film projects. In fact, when Emma's computer crashed the night before she was due to deliver a screenplay, it was her good friend and techno geek Stephen that saved the day. He stayed up all night to recover the file of *Sense and Sensibility*, which later won Emma an Oscar.

FACEBOOK

Another wildly popular social networking site, Facebook connects you not only to school friends but your most recent friends, work friends, family and even pets! It's a fantastically easy way to share news and photos that you might otherwise not get around to mentioning. You can also play online games with friends and engage in some friendly banter. Online Scrabble, anyone? If you're going to hold a party, it has an events feature that lets you put together a page for your event, manage your guest list and let people know with the click of a mouse if you're having to change the time or venue. Simple! It makes organizing lots of different groups of friends into one big bustling gang a lot easier. And you can share the photos of your great event afterwards, as long as they're not too incriminating.

TWITTER

If you want to know what Ashton Kutcher is thinking right now, then Twitter is the place to be. All it needs from you is a little blog about what you're doing and feeling every now and again, called a 'tweet'. Other 'tweeters' can follow your tweets and you can choose who to follow and receive updates from. But only throw yourself into it if you're a bit of a chatterbox in the real world too: if you can't think of much to say in the pub, chances are you'll run out of tweets pretty quickly. Updates on your choice of sandwich filling are not acceptable!

Don't Dump Your Girls

Newly-wed Scarlett Johansson knows that, however much you love your partner, your friends are a vital part of your life.

'My friends and I always talk about relationships and I always probably over-analyse everything,' she says. 'Sometimes it's nice to just vent and advise someone because you need an outside perspective. Relationships can get very sheltered and they fester in a way. So it can be nice, whether it's from your sister or your girlfriend, to get a perspective on the whole thing.'

Man's Best Friend

'A dog has lots of friends because he wags his
tail and not his tongue.'
ANONYMOUS

No book on friendship could be complete without a nod to our best friend in the animal kingdom. Dogs are unquestionably loyal and devoted pets and, unlike the oh-so-elegant cat, will turn up to see you not just at mealtimes or when they want something. Here are a few tales to remind you what a good friend a canine can be.

DOG DAYS

The richest woman in US history, Henrietta Green (1834–1916), often said that her greatest friend was her pet mongrel dog. However Hetty's visitors weren't quite so enamoured, as the dog had an unfortunate habit of biting people at will. Most of her visitors never dared complain but one friend finally spoke out against the dog and asked her to get rid of it. She refused, her final word on the subject being, 'He loves me and he doesn't know how rich I am.'

'When a man's best friend is his dog, that dog has a problem.'
EDWARD ABBEY, AMERICAN AUTHOR
AND ESSAYIST (1927–1989)

PRESIDENTIAL POOCH

President Barack Obama famously promised his two daughters, Malia and Sasha, a puppy if he made it to the White House. The family kept the US nation, some would say the world, on tenterhooks while they chose a breed. On 11 April 2009 they finally settled on a Portuguese water dog, a gift from Edward Kennedy. The puppy, christened Bo, is bound to keep the girls busy; when grown it will requires a half-hour walk every day and a swim once a week.

GREYFRIARS BOBBY

In 1858 a man named John Gray was buried in an unmarked grave in Greyfriars Kirkyard, a graveyard in the Old Town of Edinburgh. The spot became overgrown and was forgotten by all except his faithful Skye terrier, who stood guard over it for fourteen years, only leaving the grave once a day to eat. It is said that visitors to the graveyard would stand and wait for the one o'clock gun, the cue for Bobby to leave for his lunch, and the statue of Greyfriars Bobby remains the most visited monument in Edinburgh.

'Love me, love my dog.'
ENGLISH PROVERB

International Friendship Day

The first Sunday of August is International Friendship Day. This quirky little holiday officially began in the United States in 1935, when their Congress declared the first National Friendship Day, just as a one-off event. However, it was so popular it was soon being celebrated every year.

Many more countries then adopted the same date with India among the most enthusiastic participants with festivals and parties to honour the great institution of friendship.

In 1997 the United Nations named Winnie-the-Pooh, the honey-loving bear, the world's Ambassador of Friendship. And what better ambassador than a cuddly friend who happily shares his favourite sweet treat?

Celebrating this cheery holiday couldn't be easier – just spend a little extra time with your best friends. If you can't be with them, call them or email a goofy picture. And even if you are together, a card or a small gift to show how much you care about them will really be the cherry on the cake.

And why not try something different with a hint of silliness to celebrate with your best bud? You might a bit embarrassed at first, but when the giggles kick in you'll both be having a whale of the time. And if you can't look like a bit of a prat in front of your best friends, who else would put up with it?

Ideas on how to celebrate:

- Go for a retro picnic in the local park, complete with Ribena, Scotch eggs and Jaffa cakes.

- Write your pal a poem – either a funny one about your exploits or a touching one about how much she means to you. If you're stuck for inspiration, write an acrostic poem, where you write the letters of her name down the page and begin each line with that letter. But just hope she has a relatively short name!

- Dedicate a song to her on a radio station she listens to. Make it an especially cheesy one that you can dance around the kitchen to.

- Send an e-card to your closest pals, preferably one that plays a silly song when she opens it, to really make her smile.

- Make a CD of all the songs that remind you of the good times together.

- Give her a name check on your social network, declaring to all your cyber friends who your No. 1 chum is and why.

'A friend is a gift you give yourself.'
ROBERT LOUIS STEVENSON, SCOTTISH WRITER
(1850–1894)

ACKNOWLEDGEMENTS

Many thanks to Rod and Krystyna, without whom my life would
be very different, and to Andy, Nora, Sarah, Caroline,
Rob and all those I have had the privilege of calling friends.
I would also like to thank Kerry, Kate, Louise and all
at Michael O'Mara for their help and support.